I0533367

Situational Meditation Journal

Mindful Writing

ESTELLA CHAVOUS, EdD

JACINTA CHAVOUS KAMBACH, EdD

Published by
JinJin Press
The Doctoral Network
3857 Birch Street #964
Newport Beach CA 92660

All Scripture are taken from the Holy Bible, King James Version, Cambridge, 1769.

Editor: Anne C. Jacob, Popin Edits

Cover design & illustrations by: Natalia Kambach

Asst Cover, layout and design by: Ginger Marks, DocUmeant Designs
www.DocUmeantDesings.com

Library of Congress Control Number: 2025907362
ISBN: 9798218660451

This Situational Meditation Journal belongs to

_____

(*Name*)

"Meditation allows us to directly participate in our lives instead of living life as an afterthought."

~Stephen Levine

We dedicate this book to those that matter, and you know you are. Not once were we without or questioned the power of your love. It is and always will be a blessing from God that we carry on from generation to generation and throughout eternity.

CONTENTS

Welcome

Dear Reader,

Welcome. You are exactly where you need to be. Whether this is your first step into meditation or a return to yourself, The *Situational Meditation Journal* is here to walk alongside you.

There are no perfect conditions required, no special rules to follow—only your willingness to be present, just as you are. In these pages, you'll find space to breathe, reflect, and create a practice that fits your real life—full of movement, emotion, challenges, and beauty. Every moment holds the possibility for mindfulness. Every breath is an invitation back home to yourself.

Thank you for trusting me, and for trusting yourself.

We're honored to be part of your journey.

With gratitude,
Drs. Estella and Jacinta

Preface

MANY PEOPLE HESITATE TO explore meditation, believing it is tied to specific religious or spiritual traditions. Yet, in the twenty-first century—and particularly in Western culture—meditation has transcended belief systems. It is now widely recognized as a powerful tool rooted in the sciences of mental and emotional wellness, stress reduction, and positive changes in brain chemistry. Today, meditation often stands apart from religious or non-religious contexts, offering profound benefits accessible to everyone.

The *Situational Meditation Journal* is a practical guide designed to introduce you to the theory and practice behind several common forms of meditation. More importantly, it empowers you to integrate meditation into your life—on your terms. Regardless of your background or beliefs, this journal invites you to experience meditation's full range of health and wellness benefits and to make it part of your daily routine for managing stress and enhancing resilience.

The journal serves as the hands-on companion to the foundational research presented in the *Situational Meditation* book, drawing from studies such as Dr. Estella Chavous's dissertation, "Effects of Meditation Treatments in Managing Workforce Stress with Women in Leadership," and Dr. Jacinta Kambach's research on "The Effect of Music in Meditation."

But what, exactly, is *Situational Meditation*?

Situational Meditation creates a practice culture where individuals remain fully present and deeply engaged in the moment, regardless of their physical environment, emotional state, or social context. It offers limitless flexibility—allowing meditation to meet you wherever you are.

At its core, Situational Meditation is about designing a meditation practice that fits your life—whether for personal wellness, faith-based reflection, or simple everyday grounding. With the support of the entries in this journal, you will discover how to cultivate moments of peace, presence, and appreciation anytime, anywhere.

Welcome to a meditation practice without walls.

Introduction

ALL OUR LIVES, WE'VE been in a state of transformation, but not aware of that. A few years ago, a guy who had grown up in my neighborhood called to reconnect. He said, "You know, Estella, I never told you this, but you really changed my life." I was thinking, I don't even know you that well. How did I change your life? He went on to say, "You were playing kickball with your friend, and the ball rolled across the street, and you ran to get it. I was standing there, and you looked up at me and said, 'You have the most beautiful dark skin I've ever seen in my life. Your skin is like coal. It's so beautiful!' And you left." He explained, "You know, I was always teased about my color, because I was very dark. When you told me that, it changed my life." I was inspired—but also surprised.

Growing up, I was always taught that Black skin was beautiful, no matter its pigment, no matter its shade. The point is, that understanding had become part of my purpose . . . long before I even realized it. I had been living out a mission I didn't know I had been commissioned to fulfill.

That day, crossing the street, speaking honestly from my heart to that young boy—it wasn't just a moment. It was a calling. And then, decades later, getting a call from him, hearing his voice say, *"Hey Estella, how are you doing? I just want to tell you . . ."* It reminded me: purpose often reveals itself through simple, sincere acts of love.

We all have things like this happen to us. We touch people daily. What really struck me is that I had no recollection of that day or even talking to him. I remember looking at pictures a while ago of me with my family from years ago and asking myself, "Was I there?"

If I had been more focused, I may have remembered. But I was working all the time. I missed out on so much. I was a single mom, and I felt like I had to give my daughter things to keep up with everyone else. I was so busy not being focused. When I realized how much I had missed, I started pulling away from the busyness and downsizing my positions. I didn't care about my status or being a director anymore. I just wanted to be Estella.

Spending time in silence and time with my foundation of faith is when I found the true joy of life and the true joy in my transformations. That's when I started to realize my purpose. That's when I started to enjoy life. Now I create time to spend with my daughter, son-in-law, my grandchildren, family, friends and my animals.

One morning, at a payment machine, a woman asked, "How does this work?" Being that I lived in the Netherlands at that time, and my Dutch is slecht (bad), I couldn't tell her what to do. I had to be at work for a call, so I didn't have time to stop to help her. I could have said, "I'm really sorry. I really want to help you, but I have to go." But I did stop. I took the time, because that's important.

My daughter and granddaughter frequently take early morning walks. They decided to drive to the center and walk in the city. While walking, they passed a lady with no shoes. She politely said hello. Right away, their heart hurt for her. Jai asked if she had any shoes. She said no, and Jai said she looked up and saw the Virgin Mary holding Jesus and was immediately driven to ask about her shoe size. The lady told her, and Jai asked her to stay where she was. Jai walked into the nearest shoe store and asked the clerk to find an affordable, comfortable shoe. She directed her to one, purchased it, and returned it to the Lady with the shoes. The lady looked at the box and began to cry. She asked what Jai's name was, and Jai answered. She said, "Jai, you don't understand. The name of the shoe is Grace, my name! God sent you to me." The three cried with the joy of love and kindness and their purpose for that day.

That's what meditation is about, mindfulness, and love. It's all about love and caring about people and living out your purpose, known or unknown.

In the *Situational Meditation Journal*, we invite you to explore the history, origins, and benefits of some of the most common forms of meditation.

This journal serves as an introduction—not only to meditation itself but also to its powerful healing properties and its ability to support the beginning of your own personal practice.

To appreciate meditation as an art form, it's important to understand both its past and its present. This book does not claim to present all the answers, nor does it offer findings as absolute facts. Instead, it offers you a doorway: a thoughtfully curated glimpse into existing research and contemporary practices, empowering you to discover and choose the meditation path that resonates most with you.

We are writing this book with a simple but vital purpose:

- To remind you to be present.
- To encourage you to cherish the moments with your family, to step away when needed, to claim your own time with no guilt.
- To say to yourself, "I'm stepping away now—to be with my loved ones. To take a walk. To ride my bicycle, savor

a chocolate croissant, and sip a cappuccino. I have a meeting in an hour—but right now, I choose joy."

PURPOSE

We hear that word often, but living it requires presence and awareness. Our goal is to inspire you to reconnect with who you are, to listen deeply to who you wish to become, and to honor why you are here. We are writing this book to remind you:

- Take a break.
- Take the time.
- Be in the moment—so that you never forget you were here.

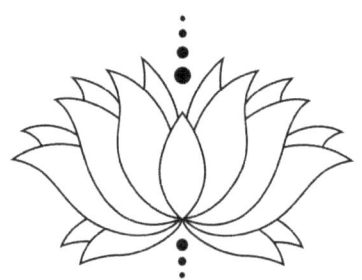

"*Situational Meditation is the art of shaping stillness to fit your life—health, heart, and purpose alike.*"

~Estella Chavous, EdD

Chapter 1:
A Background in Meditation

MANY PEOPLE WANT TO meditate but are looking for a guide, technique, or explanation to help them get started. Experiencing the love, fun, and interactions in life takes conscious awareness.

Situational Meditation is about finding this space and learning to engage in contemplation or reflection. It helps you gain back the focus on the essential things in life and manage those pressing issues clouding your mind. In short, *Situational Meditation* means that you design your situational meditation routine to make it take on whatever significance you want in your life, be it health and wellness, faith-based, both, or otherwise.

Meditation, as a practice, trains your mind to focus better on life and its purpose. Once you begin this training, you start to realize the change in your mindset with only a few minutes a day. You would also be surprised to know that meditation takes more commitment than time, so all that is needed is a ritual set toward the practice.

Ritual behavior has profound origins in humanity. It has been crucial for humans throughout history, and we still

1

need them. A ritual takes setting an intention and grounding yourself in the habit. It is effective when it is set with increased mindfulness and purpose. Being grounded takes environmental acclimation, the realization of your vision, openness to your mental capacity, utilization of the strength you have inside, and a dedication to yourself to continual change.

ORIGINS OF MEDITATION

Meditation, a practice with diverse origins and forms, has a rich history that spans religious, spiritual, and cultural roots. Its origins can be traced back to ancient times, with some suggesting that even primitive humankind used meditative states while gazing into flames of fire. The art of meditation was represented in Buddhist art as early as 500 B.C., and other countries also adopted forms of meditation based on the Hindu-based Eastern style. Meditation is not limited to Eastern cultures. Ancient Jews also practiced meditation, as demonstrated in the Old Testament scriptures in the Bible. The recent entry of meditation into the Western world has been mainly attributed to its medical benefits, and from this time to today, meditation has become popularized by Hollywood and health-focused people worldwide, leading to various adaptations in its practice. These diverse examples illustrate that meditation has a history of thousands of years and is deeply rooted in religion and spirituality.

However, despite its ancient roots in these areas, its evolution into a science designed to explore its health advantages should invite all comers to participate in its benefits, whether for religious reasons or otherwise. The body of research on meditation has found it to have positive mental and physical benefits, linking it to better overall health and improved quality of life. No matter what form of meditation is chosen, numerous cultures and religions have attested to its positive benefits throughout all practices.

THE BENEFITS OF MEDITATION

Meditation, as a Science, offers a multitude of documented benefits, from enhancing memory power to boosting creativity and, importantly, reducing stress. Its research has not only advanced treatment but also opened new horizons in the field of preventive integrative medicine. In the realm of preventive medicine, we've discovered that the root cause of many diseases is inflammation and stress, both of which can be effectively managed through meditation, providing reassurance and confidence in their potential.

One of the most intriguing aspects of alternative therapies is their potential to not only calm the mind but also influence inflammation. Research has shown that meditation can suppress the activity of genes linked to inflammation, essentially reversing molecular damage. This has been positively associated with reduced levels of C-reactive protein and other cellular inflammation markers in patients with type 2 diabetes, cancer, or heart failure, as well as in the elderly with depression and cardiovascular disease risk factors. Furthermore, those trained to meditate over eight weeks were better able to control a specific type of brain wave called alpha rhythms, which minimize distractions—suggesting its benefits in pain relief.

THE TYPES OF MEDITATION

Different types of meditation vary in origin, goal, and practice. The practices selected in this book were chosen due to the body of mainstream research. Because of this, research and experience should continue and not be limited to this book, as it is essential to continue to explore the forms that are right for you. Here is a summary of the ones we researched; more details are in the *Situational Meditation and Practice* book.

Contemplative-Centering Prayer

Contemplative-centering prayer, with its profound Christian roots, stands as a testament to the spiritual journey of every age. Its origins can be traced back to the Desert Fathers of Egypt, Palestine, and Syria. Practitioners included revered figures such as Evagrius, St. Augustine, and St. Gregory the Great in the West, and Pseudo-Dionysius and the Hesychasts in the East (contemplative Outreach). Over the first sixteen centuries of the Christian era, St. Gregory the Great eloquently described contemplative prayer as the knowledge of God, a divine fusion of scripture and God's grace.

In the twentieth and twenty-first centuries, the contemplative tradition was rekindled and enriched by the unwavering dedication of various religious orders, particularly the Jesuits and Discalced Carmelites. These orders, deeply inspired by the contemplative spirit of their founders, generously shared their spiritual wealth with laypeople. The fruit of their labor was the development of centering prayer, a practice deeply rooted in the profound wisdom of Jesus as revealed in the Sermon on the Mount.

Contemplative-centering prayer is a journey of grace, a harmonious dance with the divine presence. The ultimate goal of centering prayer is not just to be with God, but to truly experience His presence. Envision yourself in a room with pristine white walls, with your image of God before you. In Centering Prayer, your only task is to be present with God, to bask in His divine light and feel His loving embrace.

Guided Meditation

Guided meditation, a form gaining popularity across diverse populations, has its roots in contemplative, Christian, Buddhist, and other traditions. The twelfth century saw the development of meditation steps by Buddhist monks, which included reading, pondering, praying, and contemplating—tenets that continue to resonate across all practices. Whether you seek guidance from a group, a guide, or your own intuitive wisdom, you are part of a tradition that spans cultures and time.

The objectives of guided meditation are to clear the mind for relaxation, reduce stress, and foster personal and spiritual growth. Many practitioners, regardless of their religious beliefs, use guided meditation to improve their health. The techniques, which can range from calming the mind to filling it with positive imagery and affirmations, are accessible to all.

Guided meditation involves entering states of consciousness where awareness and attention are focused. A significant part of this process is the use of verbal instructions, which guide the practitioner to relax and clear the mind. This guidance provides a reassuring structure to the meditation experience.

Mindfulness Meditation

The origin of mindfulness meditation is derived from ancient Buddhist and yoga practices. It is a mental state characterized by nonjudgmental awareness, teaching people to live each moment as it unfolds. When one is mindful, one is trapped in a rigid mindset and is oblivious to context or perspective. Practitioners have adopted variations of this form of meditation specific to stress reduction. These nonreligious programs are anchored in the development of awareness in moment-to-moment experience. The goal involves focusing attention on the present circumstances and accepting them without judgment. Practitioners learn to be mindful and calm their minds.

This practice is an accepting and non-judgmental focus of one's attention on emotions, thoughts, and sensations. The focus is on an object (like breathing). Mindfulness means paying attention in a particular way: on purpose, in the present moment, and non-judgementally.

Christian Prayer Meditation

Christians often avoid meditation because they associate it with Eastern religions, but the Christian Bible is filled with examples of meditation. In the Old Testament, there are two primary Hebrew words for meditation: *Haga* (הגה), which means to utter, groan, meditate, or ponder, and *Sihach* (חיש), which means to muse, rehearse in one's mind, or contemplate. These words can also be translated as dwell, diligently consider, and heed. In the Bible, which is the word of God for Christians, the word *meditate* or the act of meditation is mentioned twenty times. Our thoughts determine our behavior, so what we think about is essential. That is why Christians believe God wants them to think about his word, which is the same thing as meditating on it. Meditation is *focused* thinking, so for Christians, the goal of meditative prayer is to focus on God's word so it can transform them into what God wants them to be. Christians should take comfort in the fact that there is guidance available for Christian meditation, whether it's through a guide who can lead you in biblical principles or the word or through silent contemplation on a sacred word, affirmation, or scripture—all done by turning the mind over to God and his word.

Transcendental Meditation

Hinduism concentrative (transcendental) meditation includes the categories of open awareness, guided practice, and mindfulness meditation. It began in the Far East and then spread to the Western world. It is based on Vedic Meditation, a simple, natural process that progressively improves the balance of the physical nervous system through regularly alternating profound restfulness with regular daily activity. Every physical activity has a corresponding mental activity, and every mental activity has a corresponding physical activity, so the body and mind are not two separate things but part of a unified whole, which should always be working in complete harmony.

Transcendental meditation is a relatively new form compared to Yoga and Buddhism. Although transcendental meditation has no religious affiliation, it did have a political association with the Natural Law Party. This political party was formed in 1992 to use the principles of meditation to find ways to solve society's problems—crime, injustice, economics, and environmental issues. Transcendental meditation is a simple technique and is not a philosophy. It is natural, simple, and effortless. It is designed to take the mind from active levels of thinking to a state of less mental activity, and its goal is to create inner peace and wellness.

As you can see, this is just a summary of each practice. *Situational Meditation* as with other forms, is your guidebook to a successful meditative practice, no matter your foundation. Understanding the history, benefits, and activities associated with the practice helps to better ground you in the form of meditation that resonates with you. Once you learn about what meditation offers, you will become more informed about the options, empowering you to choose the one that benefits you, and then your ritual can begin. No matter your choice, the act of meditation is a universal state of mind designed to enrich our faith, health, and love for ourselves and others.

MY CONTEMPLATIONS

"You can't stop the waves,
but you can learn to surf."

~Jon Kabat-Zinn

Chapter 2:
How to Meditate:
The GROUND Method

A PRIMARY GOAL OF meditation is to create change. Inability to change our behaviors and outcomes is partly due to our fear of failure and our continual attachment to something or someone. The need is to focus more on what we are wanting to experience, because many distractions pull us and cloud our thoughts. We are rarely in a present state of awareness. Meditation changes this, as it helps us focus. This allows us to grow and change by eliminating the clutter and being present in the moment. People can change when they are self-aware, receive support, and become intentional about behaving differently. But this change in mindset takes time, which sometimes feels challenging.

For example, if you have a mental health issue, or a life-long health condition that negatively impacts your attitude, habits, and behavior, it's difficult to deal with that without a tool or support to assist you. Meditation and journaling can support you in this and other challenging situations by providing timeouts that facilitate heart coherence and rebalance your nervous system, to improve your brain function, ease your anxiety, increase your self-awareness, and hone your focus.

G.R.O.U.N.D. There are many methodologies and change models that you can use to create change. And you can create your own by putting together a change management plan that includes a vision board to reflect where you are and where you want to be. In *Situational Meditation,* we have structured a change method called *GROUND*, to prepare you for your meditation practice. It can be used as a reference tool to help you reach your desired state of calm and focused intention. It looks like this:

Get Acclimated

The major environmental factors that influence meditation are time, place, space, climate, and noise. Before you begin your meditation practice, work to identify potential factors that might come into play. Try to remove the ones in your control, like closing a window, shutting a door, or silencing a cell phone. For those you can't control, first acknowledge them in your practice. After you have acknowledged them, begin to release them out of your thoughts by returning to your mantra, scripture, affirmation, breathing, or whatever focus method you have chosen.

Realize Your Vision

Most people do not visualize the place they want their practice to take them. Nothing is wrong with this, as the main goal of meditation is to go beyond the mind to a state of happiness and bliss. For us, that state of bliss is our faith. For you, it may be different. Regardless, if the mind, with all its clutter, is an obstacle to finding your bliss, a ritual of setting a vision and intentions can enhance your practice by helping you process the clutter and create the experiences you want.

Open Your Mental Capacity

When your mind thrives, you do too. Meditation has been shown to preserve the brain's gray matter by decreasing its loss, which is the cause of stress and declining health. You can contribute to the preservation of your brain by opening your mind's capacity to do so and focusing on that intention.

Use Meditation to Increase Inner Strength

You possess the innate inner fortitude to create a powerful meditative practice. As you live in your committed practice, you will be a model for others, as it will be visible in all you do. Acknowledge the change in yourself when noticed by others and let it propel you along the way. Use your meditative practice for continual growth and development, for yourself, and to support others.

Notice Wins and Conflicts

Understand your stressors and the things that prevent you from reaching the place of calm. Regardless of the source, take time to remove them from your life, or control the effects they have on you. After you incorporate this awareness and attention into your daily routine, you will be better able to calm yourself when faced with any challenge. As you experience the benefits resulting from this, acknowledge your success.

Dedicate Yourself to Continual Change and Renewal

You will experience change and renewal as you dedicate yourself to your meditation practice. It takes consistency to see continual results. This means making it a priority in your life and committing to a daily meditation routine.

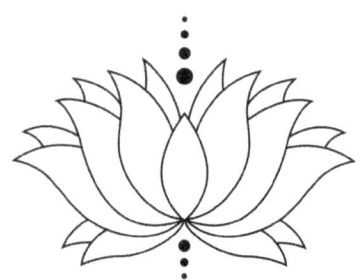

"To love yourself is to embrace the sacred stillness within, where kindness, peace and mindfulness bloom."

~Dr. Jai

Chapter 3:
How to Use the 14-Day
Situational
Mediation Journal

THANK YOU FOR CHOOSING the *Situational Mediation Journal.* We are Dr. Estella Chavous and Dr. Jacinta Kambach, and we are truly honored that you've decided to begin — or deepen — your journey of change through meditation.

As lifelong meditation practitioners, we've discovered that many people feel drawn to meditate, yet they often seek a guide, a technique, or simply a welcoming path to help them get started. This interactive guide and journal were created with you in mind.

Before you begin your guided journaling, we invite you to breathe, relax, and make this journal entirely your own. Although it begins with a fourteen-day journey, it is designed to evolve with you — to be revisited, repurposed, and expanded throughout your lifetime.

While habits can be created in as little as fourteen days, your journey is unique. There is no set pace here. The Situational Meditation Journal encourages you to embrace a situational approach to meditation — one without rigid rules or boundaries — and to cultivate a life of presence, self-love, and transformation.

This is your time. This is your space.
Welcome.

What is Situational Meditation?

Situational Meditation creates a practice culture where individuals are fully present and engaged in the moment, with appreciation and limitless constraints no matter where they are physically, emotionally, or socially. You may not be ready to commit, or have the time, to create a daily sit-down meditation practice. And that is totally ok! Meditation doesn't have to always be that. A goal of meditation is the ability to enter a state of presence, no matter what you're doing. Situation is where you are at any point in time. If you're taking a walk away from the office or through the park on Saturday morning, notice the dew on the leaves, the feel of the wet grass on the palm of your hand, the smell of the freshly cut grass, or the sound of the waterfall. Take that situation and build meditation around it. Situational Meditation allows you to step out of the outside world and monkey mind and come to a focused state of conscious awareness and appreciation. In fact, the more that you create a meditative practice in whatever situation you are in, the more calm, empowered, and centered you will become.

We also realize that everyone has a personal belief system. Your belief system has no bearing on your ability to benefit from a meditation practice. We hope you'll agree that the one ingredient that advances us, even in the smallest steps, is Love. Life is about experience and transformation. Support and Love make that possible.

The simple act of journaling—*going into a silent space where you can just be with yourself and the way you're feeling, writing down simple answers, and going with your energy*—is a meditation in itself. And that is healing. So, sometimes you may already have experienced quiet time or an awareness of something you didn't know before or treated yourself to some alone time. The time and intention you hold putting your pen to paper to write your experience or answer the prompts and questions can be a powerful meditation.

This is not to say that you have to answer each of the activities in this journal in full every time. If you're good for the day, and you got what you needed, you may want to skip one or more of the activities. You may be someone who loves to track yourself and set goals and achieve them, because it motivates you. So, you would want to do each of the activities every day. But you may be the exact opposite. The last thing you want to do is set yourself up to feel like this is a job. They're not a must do.

Just be aware of the benefit of the writing as a process of integrating transformation. Understanding and knowing in your mind is very different from integrating the knowing into your body and being. If you want to be able to let go of more, or go deeper, or transform your repetitive life themes on a core level, these activities can help you.

In our passion to put theory into practice, we developed the *Situational Meditation Journal* as a practical application focusing on the practice of Meditation. In addition to the meditations, you will also find intentions, prayers, brainstorming, brain renewals, brain clutter dumps, and mindful tips to support your practice. We hope that this results in creating a personal experience of positive change in your physical, emotional, and mental well-being

The journal includes twelve daily activities and two days for recovery. The twelve days are purposefully designed for your reflection, healing, and awareness, serving as an integral part of your journey toward peace and transformation. The seventh and fourteenth days are dedicated to *Recap, Repeat, Reflect,* and *Recover* journaling, providing you with a weekly summary of your healing progress. The act of journaling itself is a form of meditation, bringing consciousness to the areas of yourself and your life that you're not aware of or know how to change. We hope this will guide you and help you bridge this gap, keeping you focused and determined on your journey.

Days 1-6

1. Mindful Coloring—Relax Your Brain

2. Mindful Check-in—Meditation Intention

3. Beginning Your Mindful Day—Brain Renewal

4. Meditation Quote

5. Meditation Discussion & Practice

6. Beginning Your Mindful Night—Brain Clutter Dump

Day 7

1. Recap of Morning Mindful Check-in

2. Recap of Intention Setting (Starting My Day—*Not Letting it Start Me*)

3. Meditation Quote

4. Meditation Discussion & Meditation Practice

5. Personal Reflection

6. Situational Meditations

7. Observation: Letting Go

8. Observation: What was Different?

9. Observation: What was Profound?
10. Beginning Your Mindful Day
11. Beginning Your Mindful Night
12. Awareness, Shift, Healing, Resolution

Days 8–13

1. Mindful Coloring—Relax Your Brain
2. Mindful Check-in—Meditation Intention
3. Beginning Your Mindful Day—Brain Renewal
4. Meditation Quote
5. Meditation Discussion & Meditation Practice
6. Beginning Your Mindful Night—Brain Clutter Dump

Day 14

1. Recap of Morning Mindful Check-in
2. Recap of Intention Setting (Starting My Day—*Not Letting it Start Me*)
3. Meditation Quote
4. Meditation Discussion
5. Personal Reflection
6. Situational Meditations
7. Observation: Letting Go
8. Observation: What was Different?
9. Observation: What was Profound?
10. Beginning Your Mindful Day

11. Beginning Your Mindful Night

12. Awareness, Shift, Healing, Resolution

Meditation can help you find comfort in the stillness, discover loving kindness within yourself and others, restore and renew your mind, body, and spirit, bring restful bliss to your life, facilitate full body healing, and see the beauty in you and the world around you.

As you begin your *Situational Meditation Journal,* know that you deserve peace, love, and happiness. We believe this is given to us through our faith in Christ and his love. No matter what your beliefs are, you are capable of having all of it. We wish you blessings in your meditation journey.

Strategic Ladies, Jacinta and Estella
Motivate Transform Empower

MY CONTEMPLATIONS

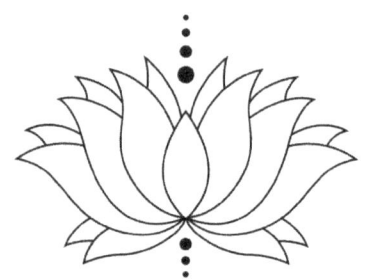

"When we are still, all settles into place. We take time to see the beauty. We take time to see the heart. And we naturally gravitate to others that resonate that inner calm. When we are still."

~Tom Althouse

Chapter 4:
Beginning Week 1: Your 14-day Meditation Journal

WEEKLY THOUGHT

What challenges, thoughts, situations of your mind, emotions, body, or life are you wanting to receive an awareness, shift, resolution, or healing? Write how you feel at the start of this journey.

....

....

....

....

....

....

....

Draw how the week feels at the start of this journey.

Mindful Coloring: "Be still."

My Contemplations

$\mathcal{D}$ay 1:
BE STILL MEDITATION
NOT DO. BE SILENT. LET GO. LISTEN.

BEING STILL CALLS YOU to take time to pause, listen, and reflect. This intentional nonaction enhances your ability to glean insight into the true nature of reality. It allows you to see things the way they are, not the way you assume they are. By not talking and not listening to noise or other communication, you create a space of quiet that allows you to hear the whisper of truth. When you stop moving, and distracting yourself in your efforts to stay busy or "*get things done*," you allow the water of your life to calm enough to see the messages in its reflection. Stillness creates the safe space for you to feel the emotions that are needing to surface in order to be felt, healed, and transmuted into inspiration. It is the space in which you can feel subtle sensations from your body and soul that are guiding you to your greater wisdom.

By being still and connecting with yourself, you can find peace amidst the chaos of life. This brings a gift that you didn't know existed and brings gratitude for the time you took for yourself and your faith in things unseen. As you meditate regularly in stillness and silence, you become more comfortable with yourself, knowing that you're being cared for, and that you don't need to race and push. Life is supporting you every step of the way.

"True silence is the rest of the mind, and is to the spirit what sleep is to the body, nourishment and refreshment."
~William Penn

27

Activity 1: Mindful Check-in: Relax Your Brain

Starting My Day—Not Letting It Start Me

Throughout the day, a good 'best practice' is to check in with yourself. Mood illustrations can be powerful tools for tracking how you feel. Be sure not to forget to check in with yourself, especially first thing in the morning, so you will start your day and not let it start you. How do you feel now?

....

....

....

....

Activity 2: Begin Your Mindful Day— Renewing Your Mind

Meditation Intention

Find a quiet place and a comfortable spot to sit or lie down. Close your eyes, take in a few deep breaths, and then return to normal breathing. Take a moment for yourself. Think about what your intention is for the day and write or draw it. Make it specific, positive, and present tense.

....

....

....

....

MORE REFLECTIVE THOUGHT

Use the suggested prompts to journal this meditation experience to create a remembrance of it for future meditations. Feel free to go beyond what is asked. Write it/Draw it.

Be Still: What does this mean to you or call you to do?

Letting go: What do you want to let go of today?

What do you want that can add to your abundance?

What time do you plan to take a situational meditation break?

Activity 3: Meditation Quote

Which quote above or that you have used in the past speaks to you most? What's your interpretation of it? What is the behavior or mindful verse/quote/mantra you will use in the presence of confusion? Focus on the behavior you want to cultivate. Write it.

....

....

....

Activity 4: Meditation Discussion & Practice

Not Do. Be Silent. Let Go. Listen.

When leading meditation at work, we sometimes incorporate breathing work and sometimes do guided meditation. We regularly lead silent meditation, a practice of sitting in silence and observing the thoughts, and contemplative prayer, a form of meditation that involves a personal relationship with a higher power. We found it interesting to see how uncomfortable the participants felt and how long they thought ten minutes was.

BEFORE THE PRACTICE

Begin your practice by finding the "Be Still" meditation you want to participate in today. You can find all the 14-themed meditations in this Journal on the Strategic Ladies (https://strategicladies.com/) site. You can also visit Calm (https://www.calm.com/) or Insight Timer (https://insight-timer.com/) for a Meditation in Stillness.

Write down the meditation you selected.

....

Prepare for the meditation by identifying a peaceful environment. Remember that focusing on the breath, sacred word, or mantra is important so you won't get distracted. Also, know that no matter what distraction comes your way, it's okay. Accept, acknowledge, and let that distraction go, focusing back on your breath, sacred word, or mantra. This practice of acceptance is an integral part of your meditation journey.

COMPLETE YOUR MINDFUL-CHECK IN

Using the Mindful Mood Faces circle/color how you feel. Write your thoughts, not in judgment but in awareness.

....

....

....

....

....

....

In today's meditative practice, we will embark on a deeply personal journey of *stillness and silence*, aiming to reach a ten-minute goal. As you meditate today, envision your own unique silent sanctuary. What does it look like? How does it make you feel? This meditation is your journey, your sanctuary. Enjoy it!

Begin the "Be Still" practice.

AFTER THE PRACTICE

Complete your Mindful-Check in.

Using the Mindful Mood Faces circle/color how you feel. Write your thoughts, not in judgment but in awareness.

....

....

....

....

....

....

....

....

....

How long did I meditate?

CIRCLE THE TIME DOT indicating the amount of time you meditated. The goal of the meditation time is to have at least ten minutes. Observe how you feel with the time you allocated to meditation but do so without judgment. What was your level of comfort with the time you spent meditating? Was it good for you? If you've done zero minutes, up your commitment just a little.

....

....

....

....

....

....

....

....

....

....

MORE REFLECTIVE THOUGHT

Use the suggested prompts to journal this meditation experience to create a remembrance of it for future meditations. Feel free to go beyond what is asked. Write it/Draw it.

What did you let go of today?

What do you notice that changed you since you've done your meditation?

Did you notice any profound thoughts or epiphanies? Did you need any help?

How will you continue this letting go throughout the day?

Activity 5: Your Mindful Night—Brain Clutter Dump

Brain dump your experience of the day. What tools, if any, did you use to let go? What tools could you have used, or might you use next time? Did you use any of the *GROUND* model (Ch 2), and if so, did it help you in your practice?

Think in terms of:

- The personal or profession situation
- The emotion you felt
- Your knee-jerk reaction
- Your desired reaction

....
....
....
....
....
....
....

Congratulate yourself with thankfulness, appreciation, and love by jotting down at least three affirmations for yourself. Example: "I am proud of myself and all that I have achieved."

1. ....

2. ....

3. ....

My Contemplations

"Loving kindness is a
profound recognition that
our lives have something
to do with one another,
that everyone counts,
everyone matters."

~Sharon Salzberg

Mindful Coloring: "Loving Kindness"

$\mathcal{D}ay$ 2:
LOVING KINDNESS MEDITATION
OPEN. NURTURE. LOVE. CHERISH.

YOU'RE NOT ONLY FASHIONED by what happens to you, but by how you continue to love through it all and how willing you are to keep opening, softening, and loving. Loving-kindness, a fundamental concept in meditation, is about being selfless, caring, and unconditionally kind to yourself and others. It's a practice that involves cultivating feelings of love and compassion towards oneself and others, and it's a key component of many meditation techniques.

Meditation is a journey that allows you to enhance your ability to forgive, connect, and have self-acceptance. The practice of loving-kindness can soften your relationships, making you more approachable and compassionate. By sharing love with others through kind acts, you can build strong social bonds, foster trust and acceptance in your relationships, and ultimately increase your overall happiness. This sense of connection can make you feel part of a larger community, enhancing your emotional well-being.

"You cannot do kindness too soon. For you never know how soon it will be too late."
~Ralph Waldo Emerson

....

....

....

Activity 1: Mindful Check-in: Relax Your Brain

Starting My Day—Not Letting It Start Me

Throughout the day, a good 'best practice' is to check in with yourself. Mood illustrations can be powerful tools for tracking how you feel. Be sure not to forget to check in with yourself, especially first thing in the morning, so you will start your day and not let it start you. How do you feel now?

....

....

....

....

Activity 2: Begin Your Mindful Day— Renewing Your Mind

Meditation Intention

Find a quiet place and a comfortable spot to sit or lie down. Close your eyes, take in a few deep breaths, and then return to normal breathing. Take a moment for yourself. Think about what your intention is for the day and write it down. Make it specific, positive, and present tense.

....

....

....

....

....

MORE REFLECTIVE THOUGHT

Use the suggested prompts to journal this meditation experience to create a remembrance of it for future meditations. Feel free to go beyond what is asked. Write it/Draw it.

Loving Kindness: What does this mean to you or call you to do?

Letting go: What do you want to let of of today?

What do you want that can add to your abundance?

What time do you plan to take a situational meditation break?

Activity 3: Meditation Quote

Which quote above or that you have used in the past speaks to you most? What's your interpretation of it? What is the behavior or mindful verse/quote/mantra you will use in the presence of confusion? Focus on the behavior you want to cultivate. Write it.

....

....

....

Activity 4: Meditation Discussion & Practice

Open. Nurture. Love. Cherish.

Being alone and not having access to the same affection or love that we're used to begins to take its toll on our mood. This lack of love makes one depressed and triggers a range of beliefs, such as worthlessness or a negative outlook on life. Some have entered our meditation sessions with a host of unresolved issues and conditions. These conditions range from hormone imbalance, mental health conditions, and post-traumatic stress disorder (PTSD), to name a few. The first thing to remember is that it is okay not to be okay, and meditation is here to give you the love and kindness you need to make connections. Meditation will help shift your thinking from negative feelings to a massive breakthrough in positive ones, breaking down that sensation of anxiety.

BEFORE THE PRACTICE

Begin your practice by finding the "Love & Kindness" meditation you want to participate in today. You can find all the 14-themed meditations in this journal on the Strategic Ladies (https://strategicladies.com/) site. You can also visit Calm (https://www.calm.

com/) or Insight Timer (https://insight-timer.com/) for a meditation in Loving Kindness.

Write down the meditation you selected.

....

....

....

....

....

....

....

Prepare for the meditation by identifying a peaceful environment. Remember that focusing on the breath, sacred word, or mantra is important so you won't get distracted. Also, know that no matter what distraction comes your way, it's okay. Accept, acknowledge, and let that distraction go, focusing back on your breath, sacred word, or mantra.

This practice of acceptance is an integral part of your meditation journey.

COMPLETE YOUR MINDFUL-CHECK IN

Using the Mindful Mood Faces circle/color how you feel. Write your thoughts, not in judgment but in awareness.

....

....

....

In today's meditative practice, you will relieve symptoms of depression and strengthen positive emotions through loving-kindness. Begin by allowing yourself time to reflect on how loving kindness feels when it is given and when you receive it. Remember to manage your feelings by acknowledging the emotion, accepting it, and letting it go. Focusing on your breaths is a key technique to bring your attention back to the present moment. Try to reach the ten-minute goal.

Begin the "Love and Kindness" practice.

AFTER THE PRACTICE

Complete your Mindful-Check in.

Using the Mindful Mood Faces circle/color how you feel. Write your thoughts, not in judgment but in awareness.

....

....

....

....

....

....

....

....

....

....

How long did I meditate?

CIRCLE THE TIME DOT and write how long your meditation was here. The goal of the meditation time is to have at least ten minutes. Circle the dot on the clock indicating the amount of time you meditated. Observe how you feel after that amount of meditation time, but do so without judgment. What was your level of comfort? Was it good for you? If you've done zero minutes, up your commitment just a little.

....

....

....

....

....

....

....

....

....

....

MORE REFLECTIVE THOUGHT

Use the suggested prompts to journal this meditation experience to create a remembrance of it for future meditations. Feel free to go beyond what is asked. Write it/Draw it.

What did you let go of today?

What do you notice that's changed in you since you've done your meditation?

Did you notice any profound thoughts or epiphanies? Did you need any help?

How will you continue this letting go throughout the day?

Activity 5: Your Mindful Night—Brain Clutter Dump

Brain dump your experience of the day. What tools, if any, did you use to let go? What tools could you have used, or might you use next time? Did you use any of the *GROUND* model (Ch 2), and if so, did it help you in your practice?

Think in terms of:

- The personal or profession situation
- The emotion you felt
- Your knee-jerk reaction
- Your desired reaction

....

....

....

....

Congratulate yourself with thankfulness, appreciation, and love by jotting down at least three affirmations for yourself. Example: "I am proud of myself and all that I have achieved."

1. ....

2. ....

3. ....

"Joy and Bliss can come from the little and most unexpected things, if only we Program our Mind to enjoy these little things."

~RVM

Mindful Coloring: "Restful Bliss"

Day 3:
RESTFUL BLISS MEDITATION
RELAX. CONNECT. KNOW. FOLLOW.

RESTFUL BLISS MEDITATIONS CAN prepare you to connect to the bliss in any part of your day, the joy you feel with your first cup of morning coffee or your relaxing herbal tea before rest. Restful bliss helps cultivate a positive mindset and know the goodness naturally present in you and your life. The challenge is recognizing when you're in the way of your own bliss, which is most of the time.

Finding personal time to reconnect with yourself and your bliss can be challenging. We say, *"Acknowledge it, accept it and let it go."* If you haven't let go before the practice, you spend more time thinking about that than being where you are in the present. Example: *"I came to this meeting, but I'm stressed out,"* or *"I've had a bad morning, and I don't really want to do this brochure,"* or *"I haven't had time to prepare, and I don't feel like it."*

If you take the time to acknowledge that you don't feel like it, you can accept that as true, feel better that you expressed it, and stop thinking about it. Letting it go allows you to engage in the activity that you didn't want to do, because you're in a different space. If you come to the practice full of stuff, your practice is going to be full of stuff—*which is okay.* But acknowledging that it's there, accepting it, and letting it go will allow your meditation to be so much more impactful and transformative for you.

When you meditate, you rest your mind and allow yourself to feel and know the natural presence of peace and rightness in the world. That is bliss.

"Rest time is not a waste. It is the economy to gather fresh strength."

~Charles Spurgeon

Activity 1: Mindful Check-in: Relax Your Brain
Starting My Day—Not Letting It Start Me

Throughout the day, a good 'best practice' is to check in with yourself. Mood illustrations can be powerful tools for tracking how you feel. Be sure not to forget to check in with yourself, especially first thing in the morning, so you will start your day and not let it start you. How do you feel now?

....

....

Activity 2: Begin Your Mindful Day— Renewing Your Mind
Meditation Intention

Find a quiet place and a comfortable spot to sit or lie down. Close your eyes, take in a few deep breaths, and then return to normal breathing. Take a moment for yourself. Think about what your intention is for the day and write it down. Make it specific, positive, and present tense.

....

....

MORE REFLECTIVE THOUGHT

Use the suggested prompts to journal this meditation experience to create a remembrance of it for future meditations. Feel free to go beyond what is asked. Write it/Draw it.

Restful Bliss: What does this mean to you or call you to do?

Letting go: What do you want to let of of today?

What do you want that can add to your abundance?

What time do you plan to take a situational meditation break?

Activity 3: Meditation Quote

Which quote above or that you have used in the past speaks to you most? What's your interpretation of it? What is the behavior or mindful verse/quote/mantra you will use in the presence of confusion? Focus on the behavior you want to cultivate. Write it.

....

....

....

Activity 4: Meditation Discussion & Practice
~Relax. Connect. Know. Follow.

I hear people at the airport talk about being stressed out and wanting something to help them relax before they get on the airplane. For some, the stress is not about the actual flight, but about where they're going and what they have to do when they get there. Some are traveling to meet family. Some are on a business trip and have to prepare. These are situations where you can practice relaxation meditation. There's more to de-stressing than sitting down and closing your eyes. Drawing, diaphragmatic breathing, and envisioning yourself happy, peaceful, or successful are a few meditation techniques to relax and allow you to feel a state of bliss. Remembering what calms you down is the first thing. Sometimes people remember what makes them stressed out, but not what calms them down. Pay attention to the methods, mindsets, and nuances that have relaxed you and created a feeling of bliss in the past.

BEFORE THE PRACTICE

Begin your practice by finding the "Restful Bliss" meditation you want to participate in today. You can find all the 14-themed meditations in this Journal on the Strategic Ladies (https://strategicladies.com/) site. You can also visit Calm (https://www.calm.com/) or Insight Timer (https://insight-timer.com/) for a meditation in Restful Bliss.

Write down the meditation you selected.

....

....

....

....

....

....

....

....

....

....

....

Prepare for the meditation by identifying a peaceful environment. Remember that focusing on the breath, sacred word, or mantra is important so you won't get distracted. Also, know that no matter what distraction comes your way, it's okay. Accept, acknowledge, and let that distraction go, focusing back on your breath, sacred word, or mantra. This practice of acceptance is an integral part of your meditation journey.

COMPLETE YOUR MINDFUL-CHECK IN

Using the Mindful Mood Faces circle/color how you feel. Write your thoughts, not in judgment but in awareness.

In this meditation, think of your "Restful Bliss". This place could be a beautiful landscape, relaxing scene, or serene animals. As you meditate today, think of your blissful place and how you can cultivate it. Whatever eases your mind, go to that place, let go, and be without judgment. Please take ten minutes to create that space and enjoy it. Continue to let go of all that doesn't serve you and focus on only what does.

Begin the "Restful Bliss" practice

AFTER THE PRACTICE

Complete your Mindful-Check in.

Using the Mindful Mood Faces circle/color how you feel. Write your thoughts, not in judgment but in awareness.

....

....

....

....

....

....

....

....

....

How long did I meditate?

CIRCLE THE TIME DOT and write how long your meditation was here. The goal of the meditation time is to have at least ten minutes. Circle the dot on the clock indicating the amount of time you meditated. Observe how you feel after that amount of meditation time, but do so without judgment. What was your level of comfort? Was it good for you? If you've done zero minutes, up your commitment just a little.

....

....

....

....

....

....

....

....

....

....

MORE REFLECTIVE THOUGHT

Use the suggested prompts to journal this meditation experience to create a remembrance of it for future meditations. Feel free to go beyond what is asked. Write it/Draw it.

What did you let go of today?

What do you notice that's changed in you since you've done your meditation?

Did you notice any profound thoughts or epiphanies? Did you need any help?

How will you continue this letting go throughout the day?

Activity 5: Your Mindful Night–Brain Clutter Dump

Brain dump your experience of the day. What tools, if any, did you use to let go? What tools could you have used, or might you use next time? Did you use any of the *GROUND* model (Ch 2), and if so, did it help you in your practice?

Think in terms of:

- The personal or profession situation
- The emotion you felt
- Your knee-jerk reaction
- Your desired reaction

....

....

Congratulate yourself with thankfulness, appreciation, and love by jotting down at least three affirmations for yourself. Example: "I am proud of myself and all that I have achieved."

1. ....

2. ....

3. ....

"The body is a self-healing organism, so it's really about clearing things out of the way so the body can heal itself."

~Barbara Brennan

Mindful Coloring: "Total Body Healing"

$\mathcal{D}ay$ 4:
TOTAL BODY HEALING MEDITATION
ASK. FEEL. BELIEVE. RECEIVE.

HOLISTIC HEALTH ENCOMPASSES THE total health of a human being in all aspects of life—physical, mental, emotional, social, and spiritual health. Your body has a tremendous ability to self-heal and regenerate from anything that is not part of your pure state.

Meditation increases your awareness of how you react to positive and negative stimuli, what you put into your body, and how you rest. Through the serenity and rejuvenated effects of meditation, your body is more attuned to eliminate stress and stimulate healthy hormones.

"Your body's ability to heal is greater than anyone has permitted you to believe."

~Carolyn Harrington

Activity 1: Mindful Check-in—Relax Your Brain
Starting My Day—Not Letting It Start Me

Throughout the day, a good 'best practice' is to check in with yourself. Mood illustrations can be powerful tools for tracking how you feel. Be sure not to forget to check in with yourself, especially first thing in the morning, so you will start your day and not let it start you. How do you feel now?

....

....

....

....

Activity 2: Begin Your Mindful Day— Renewing Your Mind
Meditation Intention

Find a quiet place and a comfortable spot to sit or lie down. Close your eyes, take in a few deep breaths, and then return to normal breathing. Take a moment for yourself. Think about what your intention is for the day and write it down. Make it specific, positive, and present tense.

....

....

....

....

....

MORE REFLECTIVE THOUGHT

Use the suggested prompts to journal this meditation experience to create a remembrance of it for future meditations. Feel free to go beyond what is asked. Write it/Draw it.

Total Body Healing: What does this mean to you or call you to do?

Letting go: What do you want to let go today?

What do you want that can add to your abundance?

What time do you plan to take a situational meditation break?

Activity 3: Meditation Quote

Which quote above or that you have used in the past speaks to you most? What's your interpretation of it? What is the behavior or mindful verse/quote/mantra you will use in the presence of confusion? Focus on the behavior you want to cultivate. Write it.

....

....

....

Activity 4: Meditation Discussion & Practice

Ask. Feel. Believe. Receive.

When we begin leading a body awareness meditation practice, we usually ask participants to *"honor their bodies"*. This means different things to different people. To us, it means to honor that our bodies are made in the image of God's likeness, by taking time to care for the mental, physical, and spiritual needs of our bodies. This can be expressed by practicing compassion, honoring your body's diversity in God's people, engaging in healthy activities, or spending time with your thoughts and emotions.

BEFORE THE PRACTICE

Begin your practice by finding the "Total Body Healing" meditation you want to participate in today. You can find all the 14-themed meditations in this Journal on the Strategic Ladies (https://strategicladies.com/) site. You can also visit Calm (https://www.calm.com/) or Insight Timer (https://insight-timer.com/) for a meditation in Total Body Healing.

Write down the meditation you selected.

....

....

Prepare for the meditation by identifying a peaceful environment. Remember that focusing on the breath, sacred word, or mantra is important so you won't get distracted. Also, know that no matter what distraction comes your way, it's okay. Accept, acknowledge, and let that distraction go, focusing back on your breath, sacred word, or mantra. This practice of acceptance is an integral part of your meditation journey.

COMPLETE YOUR MINDFUL-CHECK IN

Using the Mindful Mood Faces circle/color how you feel. Write your thoughts, not in judgment but in awareness.

....

....

....

As you meditate, take time to think about your mental health and how you will fill it with thoughts that honor it. Have an awareness of your physical body and imagine healing yourself from head to toe. Connect spiritually by having high esteem for your beliefs. Think of your body healing. You can cultivate it. Ask, feel, scan, receive, and believe.

Begin the "Total Body Healing" practice.

AFTER THE PRACTICE

Complete your Mindful-Check in.

Using the Mindful Mood Faces circle/color how you feel. Write your thoughts, not in judgment but in awareness.

....

....

....

....

....

....

....

....

....

....

How long did I meditate?

CIRCLE THE TIME DOT and write how long your meditation was here. The goal of the meditation time is to have at least ten minutes. Circle the dot on the clock indicating the amount of time you meditated. Observe how you feel after that amount of meditation time, but do so without judgment. What was your level of comfort? Was it good for you? If you've done zero minutes, up your commitment just a little.

....

....

....

....

....

....

....

....

....

....

MORE REFLECTIVE THOUGHT

Use the suggested prompts to journal this meditation experience to create a remembrance of it for future meditations. Feel free to go beyond what is asked. Write it/Draw it.

What did you let go of today?

What do you notice that changed you since you've done your meditation?

Did you notice any profound thoughts or epiphanies? Did you need any help?

How will you continue this letting go throughout the day?

Activity 5: Your Mindful Night—Brain Clutter Dump

Brain dump your experience of the day. What tools, if any, did you use to let go? What tools could you have used, or might you use next time? Did you use any of the *GROUND* model (Ch 2), and if so, did it help you in your practice?

Think in terms of:

- The personal or profession situation
- The emotion you felt
- Your knee-jerk reaction
- Your desired reaction

....

....

....

Congratulate yourself with thankfulness, appreciation, and love by jotting down at least three affirmations for yourself. Example: "I am proud of myself and all that I have achieved."

1. ....

2. ....

3. ....

MY CONTEMPLATIONS

*"If you restore balance in
your own self, you will be
contributing immensely to
the healing of the world."*

~Deepak Chopra

Mindful Coloring: "Restored & Renewed"

$\mathcal{D}ay$ 5:
RESTORED & RENEWED MEDITATION
ALLOW. REPLENISH. REBALANCE. CHANGE.

WE SEEM TO PAY more attention to things that don't serve us and don't make us happy than things that do serve us and do make us happy. To restore is to replace the areas of neglect or stress that you've added to your body and mind by focusing on things that deplete you. This restoring practice renews you and your mind, body, and spirit. Pay attention to things that serve you, that make you happy.

Understanding how to restore is a big step in managing and creating energy. It renews the strength of our mind, body, and soul. Restoration enables us to start from our original, or new foundation in life.

When you take a shower, visualize washing away your stress and anxiety. Concentrate on the feel of the water upon your skin. Envision the power of the water washing away your negative thoughts. Feel sadness, regret, anger, and depression washing right off you. Let it all go down the drain. Feel lightness in your body. Enjoy the clarity of your mind. You are free of all that does not serve your highest good. You are restored and renewed.

"Sleep is the golden chain that ties health and our bodies together."

~Thomas Dekker

Activity 1: Mindful Check-in—Relax Your Brain

Starting My Day—Not Letting It Start Me

Throughout the day, a good 'best practice' is to check in with yourself. Mood illustrations can be powerful tools for tracking how you feel. Be sure not to forget to check in with yourself, especially first thing in the morning, so you will start your day and not let it start you. How do you feel now?

....

....

....

....

Activity 2: Begin Your Mindful Day— Renewing Your Mind

Meditation Intention

Find a quiet place and a comfortable spot to sit or lie down. Close your eyes, take in a few deep breaths, and then return to normal breathing. Take a moment for yourself. Think about what your intention is for the day and write or draw it. Make it specific, positive, and present tense.

....

....

....

....

MORE REFLECTIVE THOUGHT

Use the suggested prompts to journal this meditation experience to create a remembrance of it for future meditations. Feel free to go beyond what is asked. Write it/Draw it.

Restored & Renewed: What does this mean to you or call you to do?

Letting go: What do you want to let go of today?

What do you want that can add to your abundance?

What time do you plan to take a situational meditation break?

Activity 3: Meditation Quote

Which quote above or that you have used in the past speaks to you most? What's your interpretation of it? What is the behavior or mindful verse/quote/mantra you will use in the presence of confusion? Focus on the behavior you want to cultivate. Write it.

....

....

....

Activity 4: Meditation Discussion & Practice
~Allow. Replenish. Rebalance. Change.

Can you recall an exhausting day at work, when everything seemed to go wrong, or your to-do list went differently than you planned? More was loaded on you than you anticipated, and you began to lose focus on the most straightforward of tasks. As a result, you became stressed, which affected your sleep. Your ability to renew, restore, and replenish was lost.

You've heard that you can't control what happens, but you can control how you react to it. This is a great example of a way to acknowledge that you cannot control the situation, but you can experience a healthy outcome. Take the time to pause, center yourself, and breathe through it.

BEFORE THE PRACTICE

Begin your practice by finding the "Restored & Renewed" meditation you want to participate in today. You can find all the 14-themed meditations in this Journal on the Strategic Ladies (https://strategicladies.com/) site. You can also visit Calm (https://

www.calm.com/) or Insight Timer (https://insight-timer.com/) for a meditation in Restored & Renewed.

Write down the meditation you selected.

....

....

Prepare for the meditation by identifying a peaceful environment. Remember that focusing on the breath, sacred word, or mantra is important so you won't get distracted. Also, know that no matter what distraction comes your way, it's okay. Accept, acknowledge, and let that distraction go, focusing back on your breath, sacred word, or mantra. This practice of acceptance is an integral part of your meditation journey.

COMPLETE YOUR MINDFUL-CHECK IN
Using the Mindful Mood Faces circle/color how you feel. Write your thoughts, not in judgment but in awareness.

....

....

....

In this meditation, take time to prepare yourself for winding down to sleep. Remember that the most important thing you can do for yourself is to let go of the things that don't serve you. Life will be filled with many unexpected circumstances that take you by surprise. You must learn to take a breath and focus on the things that bring you peace and joy. This will allow you to rebalance and renew your mind and behaviors. As you meditate today, think of your restoration and how you can cultivate it.

Begin the "Restored & Renewed" practice.

AFTER THE PRACTICE

Complete your Mindful-Check in.

Using the Mindful Mood Faces circle/color how you feel. Write your thoughts, not in judgment but in awareness.

....

....

....

....

....

....

....

....

....

....

How long did I meditate?

CIRCLE THE TIME DOT and write how long your meditation was here. The goal of the meditation time is to have at least ten minutes. Circle the dot on the clock indicating the amount of time you meditated. Observe how you feel after that amount of meditation time, but do so without judgment. What was your level of comfort? Was it good for you? If you've done zero minutes, up your commitment just a little.

....

....

....

....

....

....

....

....

....

....

MORE REFLECTIVE THOUGHT

Use the suggested prompts to journal this meditation experience to create a remembrance of it for future meditations. Feel free to go beyond what is asked. Write it/Draw it.

What did you let go of today?

What do you notice that changed you since you've done your meditation?

Did you notice any profound thoughts or epiphanies? Did you need any help?

How will you continue this letting go throughout the day?

Activity 5: Your Mindful Night—Brain Clutter Dump

Brain dump your experience of the day. What tools, if any, did you use to let go? What tools could you have used, or might you use next time? Did you use any of the *GROUND* model (Ch 2), and if so, did it help you in your practice?

Think in terms of:

- The personal or profession situation
- The emotion you felt
- Your knee-jerk reaction
- Your desired reaction

....

....

....

....

....

Congratulate yourself with thankfulness, appreciation, and love by jotting down at least three affirmations for yourself. Example: "I am proud of myself and all that I have achieved."

1. ....

2. ....

3. ....

MY CONTEMPLATIONS

"Sow a thought, and
you reap an act; Sow
an act, and you reap a
habit; Sow a habit, and
you reap a character;
Sow a character, and
you reap a destiny."

~John Paul Caponigro

Mindful Coloring: "Abundant Beauty"

Day 6:
ABUNDANT BEAUTY MEDITATION
PAUSE. NOTICE. APPRECIATE. BASK.

WHEN YOU HAVE TAKEN the time to slow down, nurture yourself, forgive the past, let go of the habit of struggle, and feel the beauty of you, your heart opens your eyes to the beauty all around you. Sowing that thought and action opens up a world of beauty. Beauty isn't only in perfection, nature, or scenery that takes your breath away. Beauty is everywhere, even in the heartache, chaos, and trauma. Beauty is in the crack in the sidewalk, in the short stretches of silence, in the moment when you realize something in yourself that you never knew was there.

"Beauty is when you can appreciate yourself. When you love yourself, that's when you're most beautiful."
~Zoë Kravitz

....

....

....

....

....

....

Activity 1: Mindful Check-in—Relax Your Brain

Starting My Day—Not Letting It Start Me

Throughout the day, a good 'best practice' is to check in with yourself. Mood illustrations can be powerful tools for tracking how you feel. Be sure not to forget to check in with yourself, especially first thing in the morning, so you will start your day and not let it start you. How do you feel now?

....

....

....

....

....

Activity 2: Begin Your Mindful Day—Renewing Your Mind

Meditation Intention

Find a quiet place and a comfortable spot to sit or lie down. Close your eyes, take in a few deep breaths, and then return to normal breathing. Take a moment for yourself. Think about what your intention is for the day and write or draw it. Make it specific, positive, and present tense.

....

....

....

....

MORE REFLECTIVE THOUGHT

Use the suggested prompts to journal this meditation experience to create a remembrance of it for future meditations. Feel free to go beyond what is asked. Write it/Draw it.

Abundant Beauty: What does this mean to you or call you to do?

Letting go: What do you want to let go today?

What do you want that can add to your abundance?

What time do you plan to take a situational meditation break?

Activity 3: Meditation Quote

Which quote above or that you have used in the past speaks to you most? What's your interpretation of it? What is the behavior or mindful verse/quote/mantra you will use in the presence of confusion? Focus on the behavior you want to cultivate. Write it.

....

....

....

Activity 4: Meditation Discussion & Practice

~Pause. Notice. Appreciate. Bask.

When we lived by the *Irvine Spectrum*, I couldn't run for a brief period. So, we started walking as a family. Every morning on my walk, a rabbit came out to find food and greet us, and in the same place every time. As the sun rose and lit up the day, we noticed the dew on the flowers and plants. If we had been running, the energy of our fast footsteps might have kept the rabbit from coming out. We would have been going too fast to notice the dew. The subtle natural beauty of life escapes your attention when you go too fast and don't pay attention. Creating a ritual of a slow movement allowed us to see beauty in ways I would have missed otherwise.

BEFORE THE PRACTICE

Begin your practice by finding the "Abundant Beauty" meditation you want to participate in today. You can find all the 14-themed meditations in this Journal on the Strategic Ladies (https://strategicladies.com/) site. You can also visit Calm (https://www.calm.com/) or Insight Timer (https://insight-timer.com/) for a meditation in Abundant Beauty.

Write down the meditation you selected.

....

....

Prepare for the meditation by identifying a peaceful environment. Remember that focusing on the breath, sacred word, or
mantra is important so you won't get distracted. Also, know that
no matter what distraction comes your way, it's okay. Accept,
acknowledge, and let that distraction go, focusing back on your
breath, sacred word, or mantra. This practice of acceptance is an
integral part of your meditation journey.

COMPLETE YOUR MINDFUL-CHECK IN

Using the Mindful Mood Faces circle/color how you feel. Write
your thoughts, not in judgment but in awareness.

....

....

....

....

....

As you meditate today, notice the beauty in yourself, others, and
all around you and how you can cultivate it. The meditation
allows you to experience intentionally creating a space for beauty.
It helps develop a positive mindset, focusing on the beauty
within and outside of you. It will increase all areas of Emotional
Intelligence, creating the love and happiness you deserve.

Begin the "Abundant Beauty" practice.

AFTER THE PRACTICE

Complete your Mindful-Check in.

Using the Mindful Mood Faces circle/color how you feel. Write your thoughts, not in judgment but in awareness.

How long did I meditate?

CIRCLE THE TIME DOT and write how long your meditation was here. The goal of the meditation time is to have at least ten minutes. Circle the dot on the clock indicating the amount of time you meditated. Observe how you feel after that amount of meditation time, but do so without judgment. What was your level of comfort? Was it good for you? If you've done zero minutes, up your commitment just a little.

....

....

....

....

....

....

....

....

....

....

MORE REFLECTIVE THOUGHT

Use the suggested prompts to journal this meditation experience to create a remembrance of it for future meditations. Feel free to go beyond what is asked. Write it/Draw it.

What did you let go of today?

What do you notice that changed you since you've done your meditation?

Did you notice any profound thoughts or epiphanies? Did you need any help?

How will you continue this letting go throughout the day?

Activity 5: Your Mindful Night—Brain Clutter Dump

Brain dump your experience of the day. What tools, if any, did you use to let go? What tools could you have used, or might you use next time? Did you use any of the *GROUND* model (Ch 2), and if so, did it help you in your practice?

Think in terms of:

- The personal or profession situation
- The emotion you felt
- Your knee-jerk reaction
- Your desired reaction

....

....

....

....

Congratulate yourself with thankfulness, appreciation, and love by jotting down at least three affirmations for yourself. Example: "I am proud of myself and all that I have achieved."

1. ....

2. ....

3. ....

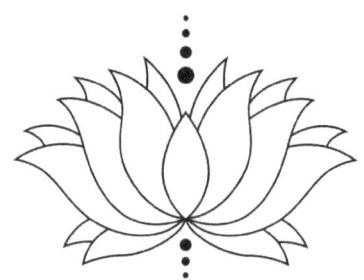

"Judge not, that ye be not judged. For with what judgment ye judge, ye shall be judged: and with what measure ye mete, it shall be measured to you again."

~Matthew 7:1–2

WEEKLY REFLECTION

CONGRATULATIONS! You made it to Day 7! This week begins by reflecting on all the manifestations and intentions experienced in your meditation practice during the previous week. It's time to recharge! You have worked really hard toward your meditation goal, and no matter where you are, take the time to process how you felt during each day of this journey. Even if you couldn't complete all the practices, journal what challenges, thoughts, situations, resolutions, emotions, body, or life experiences you received.

Write how the week felt?

....

....

....

....

....

....

....

....

....

....

....

....

....

Draw how the week felt?

"It is much more difficult to judge oneself than to judge others. If you succeed in judging yourself rightly, then you are indeed a man of true wisdom."

~Antonine de Saint- Exupery

Mindful Coloring: "Recover"

Day 7:
WEEK 1 REFLECTION
REPEAT. REFLECT. RECOVER.

ALTHOUGH WE ARE TOLD to judge or examine ourselves first and not others, this does not mean self-criticism should be a significant obstacle to our growth. It is essential to recognize when you are being too hard on yourself. We must also forgive ourselves, which is a journey, not a one-time event. It involves acknowledging our mistakes, accepting responsibility, asking for forgiveness, and practicing self-compassion. Focus on your strengths and accomplishments and set realistic expectations for growth and change. Remember, forgiveness is a journey. Be gentle with yourself and remember everyone makes mistakes. We are to love ourselves and be loved.

It is much more difficult to judge oneself than to judge others. If you succeed in judging yourself rightly, then you are indeed a man of true wisdom."
~ Antonine de Saint- Exupery

Activity 1: Mindful Check-in—Relax Your Brain

Starting My Day—Not Letting It Start Me

Throughout the day, a good 'best practice' is to check in with yourself. Mood illustrations can be powerful tools for tracking how you feel. Be sure not to forget to check in with yourself, especially first thing in the morning, so you will start your day and not let it start you. How do you feel now?

....

....

....

....

Activity 2: Begin Your Mindful Day— Renewing Your Mind

Meditation Intention

Find a quiet place and a comfortable spot to sit or lie down. Close your eyes, take in a few deep breaths, and then return to normal breathing. Take a moment for yourself. Think about what your intention is for the day and write or draw it. Make it specific, positive, and present tense.

....

....

....

....

MORE REFLECTIVE THOUGHT

Use the suggested prompts to journal this meditation experience to create a remembrance of it for future meditations. Feel free to go beyond what is asked. Write it/Draw it.

Recover: What does this mean to you or call you to do?

Letting go: What did you let go of over the entire week?

How might you continue this letting go?

What do you notice that's changed in you over the course of this week?

What were your most profound thoughts or epiphanies? Did you need any help?

....

Activity 3: Meditation Quote

Which weekly quote above or that you have used in the past speaks to you most? What's your interpretation of it? What is the behavior or mindful verse/quote/mantra you will use in the presence of confusion? Focus on the behavior you want to cultivate. Write it

....

....

....

....

....

Activity 4: Meditation Discussion & Practice

Recovery means many different things to different people. It could be an acute situation or a chronic one. Recovery goals are to return to a normal state of health, mind, or strength. As we know, normal means different things to different people. Still, for our situational meditation purpose, we mean normal to be a state of awareness and presence, allowing us to be fully engaged without being carried away by thoughts or emotions, especially those that don't serve goodness and love.

BEFORE THE PRACTICE

Begin your practice by finding a "Recovery" meditation you want to participate in today. You can find all the 14-themed meditations in this Journal on the Strategic Ladies (https://strategicladies.com/) site. You can also visit Calm (https://www.calm.com/) or Insight Timer (https://insight-timer.com/) for a meditation in Recovery.

Write down the meditation you selected.

....

....

....

....

....

....

....

....

....

....

....

....

....

....

....

....

....

Prepare for the meditation by identifying a peaceful environment. Remember that focusing on the breath, sacred word, or mantra is important so you won't get distracted. Also, know that no matter what distraction comes your way, it's okay. Accept, acknowledge, and let that distraction go, focusing back on your breath, sacred word, or mantra. This practice of acceptance is an integral part of your meditation journey.

COMPLETE YOUR MINDFUL-CHECK IN

Using the Mindful Mood Faces circle/color how you feel. Write your thoughts, not in judgment but in awareness.

....

....

....

....

....

....

....

....

In today's meditative practice, we will focus on recovery. This recovery encompasses enhancements in our mind, body, and soul. Recovery may involve prioritizing sleep, achieving a work-life balance, staying hydrated, or nourishing our bodies as needed. The essential point is that recovery is achievable if we concentrate on it, which is the experience we will embrace in today's meditation.

Begin the "Recovery" practice.

AFTER THE PRACTICE

Complete your Mindful-Check in.

Using the Mindful Mood Faces circle/color how you feel. Write your thoughts, not in judgment but in awareness.

....

....

....

....

....

....

....

....

....

....

How long did I meditate?

CIRCLE THE TIME DOT and write how long your meditation was here. The goal of the meditation time is to have at least ten minutes. Circle the dot on the clock indicating the amount of time you meditated. Observe how you feel after that amount of meditation time, but do so without judgment. What was your level of comfort? Was it good for you? If you've done zero minutes, up your commitment just a little.

....

....

....

....

....

....

....

....

....

....

MORE REFLECTIVE THOUGHT

Use the suggested prompts to journal this meditation experience to create a remembrance of it for future meditations. Feel free to go beyond what is asked. Write it/Draw it.

What did you let go of today?

What do you notice that you since you've done your meditation?

Did you notice any profound thoughts or epiphanies? Did you need any help

How will you continue this letting go throughout the day?

Activity 5: Your Mindful Night—Brain Clutter Dump

Brain dump your experience of the day. What tools, if any, did you use to let go? What tools could you have used, or might you use next time? Did you use any of the GROUND model (Ch 2), and if so, did it help you in your practice?

Think in terms of:

- The personal or profession situation
- The emotion you felt
- Your knee-jerk reaction
- Your desired reaction

....

....

....

....

....

....

Congratulate yourself with thankfulness, appreciation, and love by jotting down at least three affirmations for yourself. Example: "I am proud of myself and all that I have achieved."

1. ....

2. ....

3. ....

My Contemplations

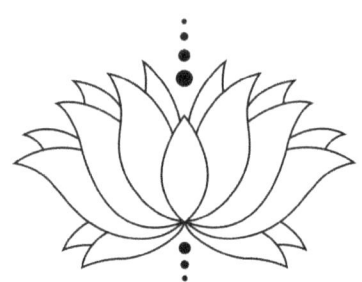

"Love is not some
accidental feeling; it is a
choice made by your heart.
That's why it makes no
sense to wait for it- it is
forever waiting for you.
Only you can switch on
the light in your heart and
decide to let love happen."

~Shei Tubali

Chapter 5:
Beginning Week 2: Your 14-day Meditation Journal

WEEKLY THOUGHT

What challenges, thoughts, situations of your mind, emotions, body, or life are you wanting to receive an awareness, shift, resolution, or healing?

Write how you feel at the start of this journey.

....

....

....

....

....

....

....

Draw how the week feel at the start of this journey.

My Contemplations

Mindful Coloring: "Universal Love"

$\mathcal{D}ay$ 8:
UNIVERSAL LOVE MEDITATION
HARMONIZE. LOVE. CONNECT.

UNIVERSAL LOVE, THE CONNECTION with everyone and everything, is a force that reinforces our uniqueness yet collectiveness. It is the dedication you have to unity and harmony among humanity. Once aligned, it takes you on a journey of connection and compassion with yourself and others. It is a calming place that allows you to open up your soul to the good around you and promotes a deep state of relaxation. Universal love is vibration and allows us to let go of anxiety and stress, understanding the meaningful purpose in our daily lives.

To fill the human heart with compassion, mercy and universal love, which should radiate to all countries, nations and peoples of the world. To make a true religion of the heart as the ruling factor in one's life.

~Kirpal Singh

....

....

....

....

....

....

....

Activity 1: Mindful Check-in—Relaxing Your Brain
Starting My Day—Not Letting It Start Me

Throughout the day, a good 'best practice' is to check in with yourself. Mood illustrations can be powerful tools for tracking how you feel. Be sure not to forget to check in with yourself, especially first thing in the morning, so you will start your day and not let it start you. How do you feel now?

....

....

....

....

Activity 2: Begin Your Mindful Day— Renewing Your Mind
Meditation Intention

Find a quiet place and a comfortable spot to sit or lie down. Close your eyes, take in a few deep breaths, and then return to normal breathing. Take a moment for yourself. Think about what your intention is for the day and write or draw it. Make it specific, positive, and present tense.

....

....

....

....

....

MORE REFLECTIVE THOUGHT

Use the suggested prompts to journal this meditation experience to create a remembrance of it for future meditations. Feel free to go beyond what is asked. Write it/Draw it.

Universal Love: What does this mean to you or call you to do?

Letting go: What do you want to let go today?

What do you want that can add to your abundance?

What time do you plan to take a situational meditation break?

Activity 3:Meditation Quote

Which quote above or that you have used in the past speaks to you most? What's your interpretation of it? What is the behavior or mindful verse/quote/mantra you will use in the presence of confusion? Focus on the behavior you want to cultivate. Write it.

....

....

....

Activity 4: Meditation Discussion & Practice

~Harmonize. Love. Connect

Harmony in a relationship means understanding; we don't need to agree to be in harmony, but we need to be willing to understand another person's experience and hear their truth. The importance here is to hear their truths. We are all diverse, and so are our belief systems. To demean and not acknowledge respectfully another truth is not love but the lack of it. Think of a challenging debate that left the two in attack mode, spilling negative thoughts or possibly even hateful words. Ultimately, this reaction is not harmonious and ultimately doesn't benefit anyone.

Conversely, try to imagine that debate is replaced by compromise or understanding. This understanding replaced negative feelings with emotions of acceptance, allowing room for differences, bridging gaps, and knowing when to let go. You see, we can only control what we can, and it is through our examples of love, harmony, and respectful disagreements, we bring about change and connection, inspiring hope and connection, possibly even toward our truths.

BEFORE THE PRACTICE

Begin your practice by finding a "Universal Love" meditation you want to participate in today. You can find all the 14-themed meditations in this Journal on the Strategic Ladies (https://strategicladies.com/) site. You can also visit Calm (https://www.calm.com/) or Insight Timer (https://insight-timer.com/) for a meditation in Universal Love.

Write down the meditation you selected

....

....

....

Prepare for the meditation by identifying a peaceful environment. Remember that focusing on the breath, sacred word, or mantra is important so you won't get distracted. Also, know that no matter what distraction comes your way, it's okay. Accept, acknowledge, and let that distraction go, focusing back on your breath, sacred word, or mantra. This practice of acceptance is an integral part of your meditation journey.

COMPLETE YOUR MINDFUL-CHECK IN

Using the Mindful Mood Faces circle/color how you feel. Write your thoughts, not in judgment but in awareness.

....

....

....

....

Today's practice will be dedicated to your "Love Nature", which refers to your innate capacity to love and empathize with others. Your love will have you act in your positive truths, which are the beliefs and values that guide your actions in a way that is beneficial and respectful to others. Opening yourself up to concern for others involves harmonizing with others not because you feel obligated but to share your true nature through love. As you meditate today, think of loving connectedness and how you can cultivate it.

Begin the "Universal Love" practice.

AFTER THE PRACTICE

Complete your Mindful-Check in.

Using the Mindful Mood Faces circle/color how you feel. Write your thoughts, not in judgment but in awareness.

....

....

....

....

....

....

....

....

....

....

How long did I meditate?

CIRCLE THE TIME DOT and write how long your meditation was here. The goal of the meditation time is to have at least ten minutes. Circle the dot on the clock indicating the amount of time you meditated. Observe how you feel after that amount of meditation time, but do so without judgment. What was your level of comfort? Was it good for you? If you've done zero minutes, up your commitment just a little.

MORE REFLECTIVE THOUGHT

Use the suggested prompts to journal this meditation experience to create a remembrance of it for future meditations. Feel free to go beyond what is asked. Write it/Draw it.

What did you let go of today?

What do you notice that changed you since you've done your meditation?

Did you notice any profound thoughts or epiphanies? Did you need any help?

How will you continue this letting go throughout the day?

Activity 5: Your Mindful Night—Brain Clutter Dump

Brain dump your experience of the day. What tools, if any, did you use to let go? What tools could you have used, or might you use next time? Did you use any of the *GROUND* model (Ch 2), (Ch 2), and if so, did it help you in your practice?

Think in terms of:

- The personal or profession situation
- The emotion you felt
- Your knee-jerk reaction
- Your desired reaction

....

....

Congratulate yourself with thankfulness, appreciation, and love by jotting down at least three affirmations for yourself. Example: "I am proud of myself and all that I have achieved."

1. ....

2. ....

3. ....

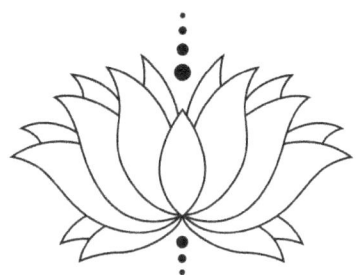

"Letting go doesn't mean forgetting, it just means we stop carrying the energy of the past into the present."

~Young Peublo

Mindful Coloring: "Gratitude"

Day 9:
LETTING GO WITH GRATITUDE MEDITATION
LET GO. CULTIVATE. EXPRESS THANKS.

WE ALL HAVE UNHELPFUL, distracting thoughts. But have you asked yourself how these are serving you? Knowing how to let go leaves your mind to focus on things that serve you. Gratitude meditation is a practice that involves reflecting on the things in life that you are grateful for and experiencing that feeling of appreciation. It can be practiced in many different ways: setting aside time to identify things that make you grateful, acknowledging something you are grateful for in real time, and writing them down for remembrance. In meditation, we do this through thought that focuses on expressing our gratitude for things in our lives, helping us cultivate a positive mindset and improve our mental well-being.

"Living in a state of gratitude is the gateway to grace" ~Arianna Huffington

Activity 1: Mindful Check-in—Relax Your Brain
Starting My Day—Not Letting It Start Me

Throughout the day, a good 'best practice' is to check in with yourself. Mood illustrations can be powerful tools for tracking how you feel. Be sure not to forget to check in with yourself, especially first thing in the morning, so you will start your day and not let it start you. How do you feel now?

....

....

....

....

Activity 2: Begin Your Mindful Day— Brain Renewal
Renewing your mind

Find a quiet place and a comfortable spot to sit or lie down. Close your eyes, take in a few deep breaths, and then return to normal breathing. Take a moment for yourself. Think about what your intention is for the day and write or draw it. Make it specific, positive, and present tense.

....

....

....

....

....

MORE REFLECTIVE THOUGHT

Use the suggested prompts to journal this meditation experience to create a remembrance of it for future meditations. Feel free to go beyond what is asked. Write it/Draw it.

Letting go with Gratitude: What does this mean to you or call you to do?

Letting go: What do you want to let go today?

What do you want that can add to your abundance?

What time do you plan to take a situational meditation break?

Activity 3: Meditation Quote

Which quote above or that you have used in the past speaks to you most? What's your interpretation of it? What is the behavior or mindful verse/quote/mantra you will use in the presence of confusion? Focus on the behavior you want to cultivate. Write it.

....

....

....

Activity 4: Meditation Discussion & Practice

Let go. Cultivate. Express thanks.

We work hard to be grateful, especially when seeing and sometimes experiencing all the suffering and chaos in the world. But it is hard sometimes to feel grateful amid trouble. A day still quite vividly in my mind reminded me to be grateful. The morning started beautifully. It was a clear, sunny California morning that went from beautiful to ugly. It started with getting soap in my eye, looking like I had pink eye, bad traffic causing my tardiness at work, and a project that took vast amounts of effort and time being caned all in one morning.

I was beside myself; rather than getting a bite to eat at lunch, I took a long walk toward a park. I sat on the nearest bench, feeling sorry for myself. After taking my hand from my head, I glanced around the park. I noticed a man walking relatively slowly and breathlessly toward me, looking like he was on his last leg. He barely reached the bench, and I immediately jumped up and asked him if he was okay. He smiled, still trying to catch his breath, but beckoned me by hand to sit down indicating he was okay.

After a few minutes, he said, Thank you for your concern. I am so grateful to be here and able to walk over to this bench. I just had my third open heart surgery, probably my last one, but it saved my life, for now. I am better each day and grateful for that. A beautiful day, wouldn't you agree, he asked.

Immediately, I was reminded of how grateful I was to walk breathlessly. That sick man on the bench reminded me of strength and how letting go is essential, no matter how big or small.

Before the Practice

Begin your practice by finding the "Letting Go with Gratitude" meditation you want to participate in today. You can find all the 14-themed meditations in this Journal on the Strategic Ladies (https://strategicladies.com/) site. You can also visit Calm (https://www.calm.com/) or Insight Timer (https://insight-timer.com/) for a meditation Letting Go with Gratitude.

Write down the meditation you selected.

....

....

....

....

....

Prepare for the meditation by identifying a peaceful environment. Remember that focusing on the breath, sacred word, or mantra is important so you won't get distracted. Also, know that no matter what distraction comes your way, it's okay. Accept, acknowledge, and let that distraction go, focusing back on your breath, sacred word, or mantra. This practice of acceptance is an integral part of your meditation journey.

COMPLETE YOUR MINDFUL-CHECK IN

Using the Mindful Mood Faces circle/color how you feel. Write your thoughts, not in judgment but in awareness.

....

....

....

In today's gratitude meditative practice, we will take a journey into the power of thankfulness. It is a practice that encourages us to let go of the past and future and fully experience the present moment. Living moment by moment is a philosophical concept and a powerful tool for promoting positive mental, physical, and social health. By acknowledging and affirming the blessings we have in our lives now, no matter how small, we can let go, cultivate, and experience the profound impact of gratefulness. As you meditate today, think of Letting go with Gratitude and how you can cultivate it.

....

....

....

....

....

....

....

Begin the "Letting Go with Gratitude" practice.

AFTER THE PRACTICE

Complete your Mindful-Check in.

Using the Mindful Mood Faces circle/color how you feel. Write your thoughts, not in judgment but in awareness.

....

....

....

....

....

....

....

How long did I meditate?

CIRCLE THE TIME DOT and write how long your meditation was here. The goal of the meditation time is to have at least ten minutes. Circle the dot on the clock indicating the amount of time you meditated. Observe how you feel after that amount of meditation time, but do so without judgment. What was your level of comfort? Was it good for you? If you've done zero minutes, up your commitment just a little.

MORE REFLECTIVE THOUGHT

Use the suggested prompts to journal this meditation experience to create a remembrance of it for future meditations. Feel free to go beyond what is asked. Write it/Draw it.

What did you let go of today?

What do you notice that's changed in you since you've done your meditation?

Did you notice any profound thoughts or epiphanies? Did you need any help?

How will you continue this letting go throughout the day?

Activity 5: Your Mindful Night—Brain Clutter Dump

Brain dump your experience of the day. What tools, if any, did you use to let go? What tools could you have used, or might you use next time? Did you use any of the *GROUND* model (Ch 2), and if so, did it help you in your practice?

Think in terms of:

- The personal or profession situation
- The emotion you felt
- Your knee-jerk reaction
- Your desired reaction

....

....

Congratulate yourself with thankfulness, appreciation, and love by jotting down at least three affirmations for yourself. Example: "I am proud of myself and all that I have achieved."

1. ....

2. ....

3. ....

*"But if you have a sacred
space and use it, eventually
something will happen.
Your sacred space is
where you find yourself
again and again."*

~Joseph Campbell

Mindful Coloring: "Sacred Space"

Day 10:
SACRED SPACE MEDITATION
WAKE. LIVE. BE.

OUR SACRED SPACES ARE aligned with our foundation. They are places of joy that come from inside, not something forced upon you. These spaces are for relaxation and self-discovery, allowing you to experience your own will, intentions, and whole self, often hidden from others. People experience sacred spaces in different ways, but there are some commonalities. Think of a sacred space as a place where you feel safe, protected, and accepted just as you are. Make the space feel like your own by choosing inspiring objects and incorporating the senses with beauty, fragrance, sound, touch, and taste; space can affect the mind and evoke different emotions. Sacred places can remind you of who you are, where you come from, and what you're about. They are a refuge free from worry, distractions, and demands, but ultimately, a place where you feel closest to me, God.

> *"Gratitude is a sacred space where you allow and know that a force greater than your ego is always at work and always available."*
>
> *~Wayne Dyer*

....

....

....

....

....

Activity 1: Mindful Check-in—Relax Your Brain

Starting My Day—Not Letting It Start Me

Throughout the day, a good 'best practice' is to check in with yourself. Mood illustrations can be powerful tools for tracking how you feel. Be sure not to forget to check in with yourself, especially first thing in the morning, so you will start your day and not let it start you. How do you feel now?

....

....

....

What is your Intention for the day? Make it specific, positive, and present tense.

....

Activity 2: Begin Your Mindful Day— Brain Renewal

Renewing your mind

Find a quiet place and a comfortable spot to sit or lie down. Close your eyes, take in a few deep breaths, and then return to normal breathing. Take a moment for yourself. Think about what your intention is for the day and write or draw it. Make it specific, positive, and present tense.

....

....

....

MORE REFLECTIVE THOUGHT

Use the suggested prompts to journal this meditation experience to create a remembrance of it for future meditations. Feel free to go beyond what is asked. Write it/Draw it.

Scared Space: What does this mean to you or call you to do?

Letting go: What do you want to let go today?

What do you want that can add to your abundance?

What time do you plan to take a situational meditation break?

Activity 3: Meditation Quote

Which quote above or that you have used in the past speaks to you most? What's your interpretation of it? What is the behavior or mindful verse/quote/mantra you will use in the presence of confusion? Focus on the behavior you want to cultivate. Write it

....

....

....

Activity 4: Meditation Discussion & Practice
~ Wake. Live. BE.

Our sacred space means different things to each of us. We all have an account of what it feels or looks like, even some who believe their sacred space is spiritual. In Genesis 2:8, Bethel, named (the House of God) is deemed a sacred space because that is where Jacob dreams of a ladder that opens the door between heaven and earth. Buddhists go on pilgrimages to places associated with Buddha's life. These places include his birthplace, Lumbini Grove, the place of enlightenment, Bodh Gaya, the place of his first sermon, Sarnath, and where he died, Kusinara. India also has many places that are considered holy, seven of which are considered to be the holiest sites in Hinduism. These sites include the holy cities of Hinduism: Kashi, Ayodhya, Mathura, Dwarka, Kanchipuram, Ujjain, and Haridwar. We share this to show that each person has a unique space and place that is sacred. It could be spiritual, like the examples I share, or simply parks, beaches, or quiet places.

Before the Practice

Begin your practice by finding the "Scared Space" meditation you want to participate in today. You can find all the 14-themed meditations in this Journal on the Strategic Ladies (https://strategicladies.com/) site. You can also visit Calm (https://www.calm.com/) or Insight Timer (https://insight-timer.com/) for a meditation in Sacred Space.

Write down the meditation you selected.

....

....

....

Prepare for the meditation by identifying a peaceful environment. Remember that focusing on the breath, sacred word, or mantra is important so you won't get distracted. Also, know that no matter what distraction comes your way, it's okay. Accept, acknowledge, and let that distraction go, focusing back on your breath, sacred word, or mantra. This practice of acceptance is an integral part of your meditation journey.

Complete your Mindful-Check in

Using the Mindful Mood Faces circle/color how you feel. Write your thoughts, not in judgment but in awareness.

....

....

....

In this meditation, you will experience a slowdown in your busy life, letting go of the overwhelming stuff. We often feel disconnected from our authentic, true, and spiritual selves. This meditation, which creates a sacred space within you, will wake you up to the present to reconnect and achieve a purpose-driven way of living and being. As you meditate today, think of your sacred space and how you will wake, live, and be in it.

Begin the "Sacred Space" Practice

AFTER THE PRACTICE

Complete your Mindful-Check in.

Using the Mindful Mood Faces circle/color how you feel. Write your thoughts, not in judgment but in awareness.

....

....

....

....

....

....

....

....

....

....

How long did I meditate?

CIRCLE THE TIME DOT and write how long your meditation was here. The goal of the meditation time is to have at least ten minutes. Circle the dot on the clock indicating the amount of time you meditated. Observe how you feel after that amount of meditation time, but do so without judgment. What was your level of comfort? Was it good for you? If you've done zero minutes, up your commitment just a little.

....

....

....

....

....

....

....

....

....

....

MORE REFLECTIVE THOUGHT

Use the suggested prompts to journal this meditation experience to create a remembrance of it for future meditations. Feel free to go beyond what is asked. Write it/Draw it.

What did you let go of today?

What do you notice that's changed in you since you've done your meditation?

Did you notice any profound thoughts or epiphanies? Did you need any help?

How will you continue this letting go throughout the day?

Activity 5: Your Mindful Night—Brain Clutter Dump

Brain dump your experience of the day. What tools, if any, did you use to let go? What tools could you have used, or might you use next time? Did you use any of the *GROUND* model (Ch 2), and if so, did it help you in your practice?

Think in terms of:

- The personal or profession situation
- The emotion you felt
- Your knee-jerk reaction
- Your desired reaction

....

....

....

Congratulate yourself with thankfulness, appreciation, and love by jotting down at least three affirmations for yourself. Example: "I am proud of myself and all that I have achieved."

1. ....

2. ....

3. ....

"Self-Love is a constant
choice. It's not a magical
feeling that appears to you
one day. It's a commitment
to your boundaries,
your well-being, your
mental and emotional
health, and your body."

~Tiny Buddha

Mindful Coloring: "Self-Love"

$\mathcal{D}ay$ 11:
SELF-LOVE MEDITATION
PEACE. WORTH. ENOUGH.

SELF-LOVE, THE ACT OF valuing your wellbeing and happiness, is a concept that can guide you to peace, self-worth, and knowing that you are enough. It's not about sacrificing your needs to please others, but rather a state of appreciation for yourself that grows from your actions in supporting your physical, psychological, and spiritual growth, resulting in overall wellbeing. Understanding and practicing self-love can inspire you and boost your confidence. Self-love is a positive trait that involves having a good understanding of yourself and treating yourself with kindness and appreciation. It's a journey that can take time to develop but can positively impact your mental and physical wellbeing.

"Until you love yourself, you will never know who you really are and you won't know what you're really capable of."

153

Activity 1: Mindful Check-in—Relax Your Brain
Starting My Day—Not Letting It Start Me

Throughout the day, a good 'best practice' is to check in with yourself. Mood illustrations can be powerful tools for tracking how you feel. Be sure not to forget to check in with yourself, especially first thing in the morning, so you will start your day and not let it start you. How do you feel now?

....

....

....

....

....

Activity 2: Your Mindful Day—Brain Renewal
Renewing your mind

Find a quiet place and a comfortable spot to sit or lie down. Close your eyes, take in a few deep breaths, and then return to normal breathing. Take a moment for yourself. Think about what your intention is for the day and write or draw it. Make it specific, positive, and present tense.

....

....

....

....

....

MORE REFLECTIVE THOUGHT

Use the suggested prompts to journal this meditation experience to create a remembrance of it for future meditations. Feel free to go beyond what is asked. Write it/Draw it.

Self Love: What does this
mean to you or call you to do?

Letting go: What do you want
to let go today?

What do you want that can
add to your abundance?

What time do you plan to
take a situational meditation break?

Activity 3: Meditation Quote

Which quote above or that you have used in the past speaks to you most? What's your interpretation of it? What is the behavior or mindful verse/quote/mantra you will use in the presence of confusion? Focus on the behavior you want to cultivate. Write it.

....

....

....

Activity 4: Meditation Discussion & Practice

~Peace. Worth. Enough.

We all have accounts reminding us of how we were without peace, worth, or feeling we were enough. My remembrance of this was as a high school student with severe acne and scarring. I had very few friends, much of whom I could never depend on. During that time, I thought my self-worth revolved around my likes, the number of invites I got to events, and my looks, which I hated because of my complexion. I can remember someone who was a friend of my brothers taking me on and unmasking all the makeup I used to cover my scars. She made me feel better about myself and helped me build confidence by accepting my looks and seeing my inner beauty despite my flaws. Once I stepped back and realized that I didn't have to be perfect to love myself, I began to gain acceptance and even be awarded a seat in the prom court. I share this to show that beauty is within, and once you love yourself, you can share that love with others. Remember, it's not about changing yourself to fit in, but about loving yourself and attracting the right people into your life.

BEFORE THE PRACTICE

Begin your practice by finding the "Self-Love" meditation you want to participate in today. You can find all the 14-themed meditations in this Journal on the Strategic Ladies (https://strategicladies.com/) site. You can also visit Calm (https://www.calm.com/) or Insight Timer (https://insight-timer.com/) for a meditation in Self-Love

Write down the meditation you selected.

....

....

....

....

....

....

....

....

....

....

....

Prepare for the meditation by identifying a peaceful environment. Remember that focusing on the breath, sacred word, or mantra is important so you won't get distracted. Also, know that no matter what distraction comes your way, it's okay. Accept, acknowledge, and let that distraction go, focusing back on your breath, sacred word, or mantra. This practice of acceptance is an integral part of your meditation journey.

COMPLETE YOUR MINDFUL-CHECK IN

Using the Mindful Mood Faces circle/color how you feel. Write your thoughts, not in judgment but in awareness.

....

....

....

In today's meditation, you will experience "Self-love", a powerful tool that will bring awareness to self-love and teach us to love ourselves truly. It will allow us to experience the peace and self-worth we deserve. You are enough no matter the circumstance or how you look in this situation. This meditation will guide you in your journey towards self-acceptance, providing the support and encouragement you need to love yourself unconditionally. Remember, that you are worthy of peace, worth, and how you are enough.

....

....

....

....

....

....

....

Begin the "Self-Love" Practice

AFTER THE PRACTICE

Complete your Mindful-Check in.

Using the Mindful Mood Faces circle/color how you feel. Write your thoughts, not in judgment but in awareness.

....

....

....

....

....

....

....

....

....

....

How long did I meditate?

CIRCLE THE TIME DOT and write how long your meditation was here. The goal of the meditation time is to have at least ten minutes. Circle the dot on the clock indicating the amount of time you meditated. Observe how you feel after that amount of meditation time, but do so without judgment. What was your level of comfort? Was it good for you? If you've done zero minutes, up your commitment just a little.

....

....

....

....

....

....

....

....

....

....

MORE REFLECTIVE THOUGHT

Use the suggested prompts to journal this meditation experience to create a remembrance of it for future meditations. Feel free to go beyond what is asked. Write it/Draw it.

What did you let go of today?

What do you notice that's changed in you since you've done your meditation?

Did you notice any profound thoughts or epiphanies? Did you need any help?

How will you continue this letting go throughout the day?

Activity 5: Your Mindful Night—Brain Clutter Dump

Brain dump your experience of the day. What tools, if any, did you use to let go? What tools could you have used, or might you use next time? Did you use any of the *GROUND* model (Ch 2), and if so, did it help you in your practice?

Think in terms of:

- The personal or profession situation
- The emotion you felt
- Your knee-jerk reaction
- Your desired reaction

....

....

....

Congratulate yourself with thankfulness, appreciation, and love by jotting down at least three affirmations for yourself. Example: "I am proud of myself and all that I have achieved."

1. ....

2. ....

3. ....

"I learned that courage was not the absence of fear, but the triumph over it. The brave man is not he who does not feel afraid, but he who conquers that fear."

~Nelson Mandela

Mindful Coloring: "Building Courage"

Day 12:
BUILDING COURAGE MEDITATION
CONTROL. MANAGE. BUILD.

COURAGE IS THE MENTAL or moral strength to persevere and withstand danger, fear, or difficulty. Most philosophers and psychologists agree that courage involves persistence in danger or hardship. However, some argue that courage is synonymous with fearlessness, while others suggest that the presence or the absence of fear has nothing to do with courage. Regardless of the thought on this, courage is the ability to do something that frightens and find strength in the face of grief and pain. Meditation is a powerful tool for building courage as it will help you step into your courage and take action on all those scary things in life. It will help you know that you have everything it takes to create the life you want to live. Meditation, a beacon of hope, can help build courage and inner strength, and guided meditation can help with this.

"We must build dikes of courage to hold back the flood of fear."

—Martin Luther King, Jr.

....

....

....

....

Activity 1: Mindful Check-in—Relax Your Brain
Starting My Day—Not Letting It Start Me

Throughout the day, a good 'best practice' is to check in with yourself. Mood illustrations can be powerful tools for tracking how you feel. Be sure not to forget to check in with yourself, especially first thing in the morning, so you will start your day and not let it start you. How do you feel now?

....

....

....

....

....

Activity 2: Your Mindful Day—Renewing Your Mind
Meditation Intention

Find a quiet place and a comfortable spot to sit or lie down. Close your eyes, take in a few deep breaths, and then return to normal breathing. Take a moment for yourself. Think about what your intention is for the day and write or draw it. Make it specific, positive, and present tense. Letting go: What do you want to let go today?

....

....

....

....

MORE REFLECTIVE THOUGHT

Use the suggested prompts to journal this meditation experience to create a remembrance of it for future meditations. Feel free to go beyond what is asked. Write it/Draw it.

Building Courage: What does this mean to you or call you to do?

Letting Go: What do you want to let go of today?

What do you want that can add to your abundance?

What time do you plan to take a situational meditation break?

Activity 3: Meditation Quote

Which quote above or that you have used in the past speaks to you most? What's your interpretation of it? What is the behavior or mindful verse/quote/mantra you will use in the presence of confusion? Focus on the behavior you want to cultivate. Write it.

....

....

....

Activity 4: Meditation Discussion & Practice

Control. Manage. Build.

One of the most remarkable testimonies of courage is our stepping into and facing what we fear. There are many stories of courage, including those from history, the Bible, and everyday life. Lt. Kennedy and his crew were rammed by a Japanese destroyer while in combat near the Solomon Islands. Kennedy dove into the burning oil to rescue three men, and he and the remaining crew members clung to the wreckage for twelve hours. Lock is another example as he shot down two German aircraft in one patrol during the Battle of Britain. He was awarded a Bar to the Distinguished Flying Cross for his actions. In the Bible, Jeremiah was imprisoned, beaten, and ridiculed by people who plotted against him, but he continued to speak the truth for about 40 years. All of these are heroic testimonies to courage but the simple act of tying your shoes, learning to ride a bike, and managing fear are everyday examples of courage that, although seeming small, are very big to someone new to the challenge. Meditation can help train the brain to break the cycle of negative self-talk that can lead to anxiety and loss of confidence. Regular meditation practice increases awareness of each moment, regardless of its pleasantness or unpleasantness. Gradually, the mind becomes comfortable with fear and other emotions, and we stop resisting them. Innate courage, an aspect of our inner being, shines through so we can control, manage, and build it, as seen in earlier testimonies.

Before the Practice

Begin your practice by finding the "Building Courage" meditation you want to participate in today. You can find all the 14-themed meditations in this Journal on the Strategic Ladies (https://strategicladies.com/) site. You can also visit Calm (https://www.calm.com/) or Insight Timer (https://insight-timer.com/) for a Meditation in Building Courage.

Write down the meditation you selected.

....

....

....

....

....

....

....

Prepare for the meditation by identifying a peaceful environment. Remember that focusing on the breath, sacred word, or mantra is important so you won't get distracted. Also, know that no matter what distraction comes your way, it's okay. Accept, acknowledge, and let that distraction go, focusing back on your breath, sacred word, or mantra. This practice of acceptance is an integral part of your meditation journey.

COMPLETE YOUR MINDFUL-CHECK IN

Using the Mindful Mood Faces circle/color how you feel. Write your thoughts, not in judgment but in awareness.

....

....

....

In today's meditation, you will reflect on courage, your ability to let go of something that frightens you, and your strength in the face of grief and pain. This meditation will help you step into your courage and take action on all those scary things in life. It will instill in you the belief that you have the power to create the life you want to live. As you meditate today, think of Building Courage and how you can Control, Manage and Build it.

....

....

....

....

....

....

....

....

....

Begin the "Building Courage" Practice

AFTER THE PRACTICE

Complete your Mindful-Check in.

Using the Mindful Mood Faces circle/color how you feel. Write your thoughts, not in judgment but in awareness.

....

....

....

....

....

....

....

....

....

....

How long did I meditate?

CIRCLE THE TIME DOT and write how long your meditation was here. The goal of the meditation time is to have at least ten minutes. Circle the dot on the clock indicating the amount of time you meditated. Observe how you feel after that amount of meditation time, but do so without judgment. What was your level of comfort? Was it good for you? If you've done zero minutes, up your commitment just a little.

....

....

....

....

....

....

....

....

....

....

MORE REFLECTIVE THOUGHT

Use the suggested prompts to journal this meditation experience to create a remembrance of it for future meditations. Feel free to go beyond what is asked. Write it/Draw it.

What did you let go of today?

What do you notice that's changed in you since you've done your meditation?

Did you notice any profound thoughts or epiphanies? Did you need any help?

How will you continue this letting go throughout the day?

Activity 5: Your Mindful Night–Brain Clutter Dump

Brain dump your experience of the day. What tools, if any, did you use to let go? What tools could you have used, or might you use next time? Did you use any of the *GROUND* model (Ch2), and if so, did it help you in your practice?

Think in terms of:

- The personal or profession situation
- The emotion you felt
- Your knee-jerk reaction
- Your desired reaction

....

....

....

Congratulate yourself with thankfulness, appreciation, and love by jotting down at least three affirmations for yourself. Example: "I am proud of myself and all that I have achieved."

1. ....

2. ....

3. ....

"Awareness is like the sun,
When it shines on things,
they are transformed."

~Thich Nhat Hanh

Mindful Coloring: "Being Fully Present"

Day 13:
BEING FULLY PRESENT MEDITATION
RELEASE. EMBRACE. OBSERVE.

OUR MINDS ARE A space for thoughts. Thoughts come and go, but controlling them can be challenging at times. When you use the word present, it means that you are aware and just observing. It is a state of mind, not position. Being in the present moment, or the "here and now," means that we are aware and mindful of what is happening at this very moment. We are not distracted by past or future worries; we are present in the here and now. This mental context allows us to control our life in every aspect with respect to action. When present, you focus on what you're doing rather than what you're not doing. These practices bring you into the present moment and have been proven to decrease worry and anxiety, allowing for release, embrace, and observation.

"Living in the moment means letting go of the past and not waiting for the future. It means living your life consciously, aware that each moment you breathe is a gift."

~Oprah Winfrey.

Activity 1: Mindful Check-in—Relax Your Brain
Starting My Day—Not Letting It Start Me

Throughout the day, a good 'best practice' is to check in with yourself. Mood illustrations can be powerful tools for tracking how you feel. Be sure not to forget to check in with yourself, especially first thing in the morning, so you will start your day and not let it start you. How do you feel now?

....

....

....

What is your Intention for the day? Make it specific, positive, and present tense.

....

Activity 2: Begin Your Mindful Day—Renewing Your Mind
Meditation Intention

Find a quiet place and a comfortable spot to sit or lie down. Close your eyes, take in a few deep breaths, and then return to normal breathing. Take a moment for yourself. Think about what your intention is for the day and write or draw it. Make it specific, positive, and present tense.

....

....

....

MORE REFLECTIVE THOUGHT

Use the suggested prompts to journal this meditation experience to create a remembrance of it for future meditations. Feel free to go beyond what is asked. Write it/Draw it.

Being Fully Present: What does this mean to you or call you to do?

Letting go: What do you want to let go today?

What do you want that can add to your abundance?

What time do you plan to take a situational meditation break?

Activity 3: Meditation Quote

Which quote above or that you have used in the past speaks to you most? What's your interpretation of it? What is the behavior or mindful verse/quote/mantra you will use in the presence of confusion? Focus on the behavior you want to cultivate. Write it.

....

....

....

....

Activity 4: Meditation Discussion & Practice

~Release. Embrace. Observe.

There are many ways to be present in the moment, but with all the distractions, it is only possible with focused attention. I can share countless stories about not being focused, but one famous illustration that comes to mind sums it up nicely. This illustration visualizes mindfulness and shows a dog and its owner walking him. The bubble outlining the dog's thoughts shows him focusing on what he sees on his walk. The dog is Mindful. The other bubble above his owner is full of clutter, which expresses all the stuff in his head, and he is Mindful.

Before the Practice

Begin your practice by finding the "Being Fully Present" meditation you want to participate in today. You can find all the 14-themed meditations in this Journal on the Strategic Ladies (https://strategicladies.com/) site. You can also visit Calm (https://www.calm.com/) or Insight Timer (https://insight-timer.com/) for a meditation in Being Fully Present.

Write down the meditation you selected.

....

....

....

....

....

Prepare for the meditation by identifying a peaceful environment. Remember that focusing on the breath, sacred word, or mantra is important so you won't get distracted. Also, know that no matter what distraction comes your way, it's okay. Accept, acknowledge, and let that distraction go, focusing back on your breath, sacred word, or mantra. This practice of acceptance is an integral part of your meditation journey.

COMPLETE YOUR MINDFUL-CHECK IN

Using the Mindful Mood Faces circle/color how you feel. Write your thoughts, not in judgment but in awareness.

....

....

....

....

....

....

....

In today's meditative practice, we will constantly observe ourselves and visitors who enter our thoughts. A goal in this meditation is to let go of all that takes you away from focus and bring that focus back to you to gain better clarity, receptivity, and alertness through less mind clutter. As you dive deeper into this aspect of meditation, you will see benefits in better clarity and receptivity, attention, thoughtless mind, and acceptance. As you meditate today, focus on the concept of "Being Fully Present", which is the core principle of mindfulness. Understand how to Release, Embrace, and Observe it.

....

....

....

....

....

....

....

....

....

....

....

....

....

....

....

Begin the "Being Fully Present" Practice

AFTER THE PRACTICE

Complete your Mindful-Check in.

Using the Mindful Mood Faces circle/color how you feel. Write your thoughts, not in judgment but in awareness.

....

....

....

....

....

....

....

....

....

BEGIN THE PRACTICE

How long did I meditate?

CIRCLE THE TIME DOT and write how long your meditation was here. The goal of the meditation time is to have at least ten minutes. Circle the dot on the clock indicating the amount of time you meditated. Observe how you feel after that amount of meditation time, but do so without judgment. What was your level of comfort? Was it good for you? If you've done zero minutes, up your commitment just a little.

....

....

....

....

....

....

....

....

....

More Reflective Thought

Use the suggested prompts to journal this meditation experience to create a remembrance of it for future meditations. Feel free to go beyond what is asked. Write it/Draw it.

What did you let go of today?

What do you notice that's changed in you since you've done your meditation?

Did you notice any profound thoughts or epiphanies? Did you need any help?

How will you continue this letting go throughout the day?

Activity 5: Your Mindful Night—Brain Clutter Dump

Brain dump your experience of the day. What tools, if any, did you use to let go? What tools could you have used, or might you use next time? Did you use any of the *GROUND* model (Ch 2), and if so, did it help you in your practice?

Think in terms of:

- The personal or profession situation
- The emotion you felt
- Your knee-jerk reaction
- Your desired reaction

....

....

....

Congratulate yourself with thankfulness, appreciation, and love by jotting down at least three affirmations for yourself. Example: "I am proud of myself and all that I have achieved."

1. ....

2. ....

3. ....

"The way I see it is if you want the rainbow, you have to put up with the rain."

~Dolly Parton

Mindful Color "Recovery"

Day 14:
WEEK 2 REFLECTION
REPEAT. REFLECT. RECOVER.

CONGRATULATIONS ON DAY 14! Your commencement Day! Reflect on the past 13 days, where you've dedicated yourself to building a habit that will enable you to fully engage with the present moment every day. This is a significant step toward training your mind to be more present and creating positive change. Take a moment to bask in your progress and feel proud of your accomplishment: this is a true testament to your success.

It's time to recharge. You have worked really hard toward your meditation goal, and no matter where you are, take time to process how you feel during each day of this journey. You have experienced many benefits during the weeks you embarked on the meditation journey, possibly in stress reduction, lower anxiety levels, better sleep, or increased self-awareness. You may not realize this, but your meditation has shifted your thinking from negative thoughts that feel too intense to ones of awareness, which is healing. Continue this journey because meditation practices can help you observe your mind and recognize its tendency to wander, creating a renewed space of focus and peace.

"The journey of a thousand miles begins with a single step ."
~ Lao Tzu

....

....

Activity 1: Mindful Check-in—Relax Your Brain
Starting My Day—Not Letting It Start Me

Throughout the day, a good 'best practice' is to check in with yourself. Mood illustrations can be powerful tools for tracking how you feel. Be sure not to forget to check in with yourself, especially first thing in the morning, so you will start your day and not let it start you. How do you feel now?

....

....

....

....

Activity 2: Begin Your Mindful Day— Renewing Your Mind
Meditation Intention

Find a quiet place and a comfortable spot to sit or lie down. Close your eyes, take in a few deep breaths, and then return to normal breathing. Take a moment for yourself. Think about what your intention is for the day and write or draw it. Make it specific, positive, and present tense.

....

....

....

....

MORE REFLECTIVE THOUGHT

Use the suggested prompts to journal this meditation experience to create a remembrance of it for future meditations. Feel free to go beyond what is asked. Write it/Draw it.

Recovery: What does this mean to you or call you to do?

Letting go: What did you let go of over the entire week?

How might you continue this letting go?

What do you notice that's changed in you over the course of this week?

What were your most pro-
found thoughts or epiphanies?
Did you need any help?

....

Activity 3: Meditation Quote

Which weekly quote above or that you have used in the past
speaks to you most? What's your interpretation of it? What is
the behavior or mindful verse/quote/mantra you will use in the
presence of confusion? Focus on the behavior you want to cultivate. Write it.

....

....

....

Activity 4: Meditation Discussion & Practice

Recover

You have reached your commencement, representing the completion of our 14-day meditation practice. It is the time to
celebrate your dedication to the practice and look to a new life
full of mindfulness. Through this 14-day practice, I am sure life
presented you with challenges. Some may seem like receiving
a lemon, and others like distractions, getting in your way. The
important thing is that we prepare our mindset to face adversity
and challenges, turning them into actions that propel us forward.

Meditation is a practice that helps us acknowledge situations, accept them, and let them go so our focus can be on the present and the now. Don't stop this 14-day practice; instead, continue to go back again and again—a commitment to meditation can turn setbacks into better solutions for our well-being.

BEFORE THE PRACTICE

Begin your practice by finding a "Recovery" meditation you want to participate in today. You can find all the 14-themed meditations in this Journal on the Strategic Ladies (https://strategicladies.com/) site. You can also visit Calm (https://www.calm.com/) or Insight Timer (https://insight-timer.com/) for a Meditation in Recovery.

Write down the meditation you selected.

....

....

....

....

....

....

....

....

Prepare for the meditation by identifying a peaceful environment. Remember that focusing on the breath, sacred word, or mantra is important so you won't get distracted. Also, know that no matter what distraction comes your way, it's okay. Accept, acknowledge, and let that distraction go, focusing back on your breath, sacred word, or mantra. This practice of acceptance is an integral part of your meditation journey.

COMPLETE YOUR MINDFUL-CHECK IN

Using the Mindful Mood Faces circle/color how you feel. Write your thoughts, not in judgment but in awareness.

....

....

....

....

....

In today's meditative practice, we will constantly observe ourselves and visitors who enter our thoughts. As you have learned, a goal in meditation is to let go of all that takes you away from focus and bring that focus back to you to gain better clarity, receptivity, and alertness through less mind clutter. As you dive deeper into the recovery aspect of meditation, you will see benefits. No recovery session is the same, so Release, Embrace, and Observe the experience.

....

....

....

....

....

Begin the "Recovery" Practice

AFTER THE PRACTICE

Complete your Mindful-Check in.

Using the Mindful Mood Faces circle/color how you feel. Write your thoughts, not in judgment but in awareness.

....

....

....

....

....

....

....

....

....

BEGIN THE PRACTICE

How long did I meditate?

CIRCLE THE TIME DOT and write how long your meditation was here. The goal of the meditation time is to have at least ten minutes. Circle the dot on the clock indicating the amount of time you meditated. Observe how you feel after that amount of meditation time, but do so without judgment. What was your level of comfort? Was it good for you? If you've done zero minutes, up your commitment just a little.

....

....

....

....

....

....

....

....

....

MORE REFLECTIVE THOUGHT

Use the suggested prompts to journal this meditation experience to create a remembrance of it for future meditations. Feel free to go beyond what is asked. Write it/Draw it.

What did you let go of today?

What do you notice that changed you since you've done your meditation?

Did you notice any profound thoughts or epiphanies? Did you need any help?

How will you continue this letting go throughout the day?

Activity 5: Your Mindful Night—Brain Clutter Dump

Brain dump your experience of the day. What tools, if any, did you use to let go? What tools could you have used, or might you use next time? Did you use any of the GROUND model (Ch 2), and if so, did it help you in your practice?

Think in terms of:

- The personal or profession situation
- The emotion you felt
- Your knee-jerk reaction
- Your desired reaction

....

....

....

Congratulate yourself with thankfulness, appreciation and love by jotting down a few weekly affirmations for yourself. Example: "I am proud of myself and all that I have achieved."

1. ....

2. ....

3. ....

MY CONTEMPLATIONS

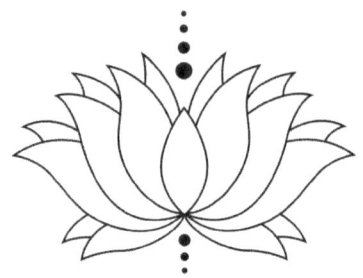

"*Situational Meditation reminds us: Awareness is the gateway to joy, love, and living fully present.*"

~Situational Meditation Journal

How to Continue the Benefits and Transformative Shifts of Your Situational Meditation Practice

THIS IS NOT THE end; it is the beginning!

While this marks the completion of your 14-day Situational Meditation practice, it is truly just the beginning. As you move forward, you will continue to experience meditation's deep and lasting benefits through knowledge and practice. Over time, meditation has been shown to improve sleep quality, regulate the central nervous system, reduce and even prevent stress, and cultivate a sense of daily fulfillment and gratitude.

This requires us to regularly check in with ourselves through meditation to deepen our awareness of the changes we can embrace to live more authentically and align with our truest selves. Meditation awakens a greater consciousness, revealing what was once hidden and opening the path to deeper understanding. In this unfolding, we come to know who we are truly. Your journey of self-discovery and connection is only just beginning.

You see, understanding the true meaning of meditation has only recently been understood. You do not have to go to a mountaintop to meditate—*but you can*. Nor do you need to sit with your eyes closed in a lotus pose—*but you can*. You don't need to sit for an hour in the solitude of your bedroom—*but you can*. Meditation is not an activity you do only at the beginning of your day or before you sleep—*but it can be*. It is not something you need to plan if you want to do it—*but you can*. Meditation requires no structure, mantras, belief, religion, or particular environment—*but it can*. It can be all of these or none of these. The freedom and flexibility of meditation are yours to explore and embrace. And remember, meditation is a deeply personal practice. You're putting your whole self into it opens us up to a practical personal experience unique to only you.

Now that you have this newfound awareness of meditation, do not confined it to a specific time or place. It can be seamlessly integrated into your daily activities, whether you're walking, bathing, cooking, or cleaning your house. It's present when you're petting your cat, gardening, singing, exercising, or journaling. It's there when you're preparing a speech or a new project or sitting in prayer. There's no right way to meditate because it's about being with your soul and your higher power. Meditation is the space you go to that connects you with your heart. It's the place in you that has always been and always will be. Your only task is to connect with it.

Meditation brings you to your natural state, the state you were in as a child before you were inundated with the conditioned rights and wrongs the world taught. Regardless of your situation, remember that you can take time out of the outside world and connect with yourself, even if it's for five minutes.

How can this meditation journal contribute to you after you have finished it or paused midway?

Whether you jot down a little in your journal or if you miss a day, each entry reflects a unique moment in your life. Building a habit of journaling is a journey that requires consistency, patience, and a fun experience. Our goal is not just to fill the pages of your journal with images, text, mantras, quotes, and colors, but to help you appreciate the journey and the progress you make along the way.

Start small, schedule time, find your comfortable space, or experiment with a prompt like the ones given to you in this journal, or make up your own. All of this contributes to the development of a pre-journaling routine, a consistent ritual that you can adapt and adjust to suit your needs and preferences. This adaptability empowers you to take control of your journaling practice. When a situation throws you out of balance and causes emotional stress, journaling can be a way to heal yourself quickly.

Life has a way of repeating its lessons until we learn from them. If you find yourself facing the same challenges or themes in different situations, it's a sign that you are being asked to make a more profound change. By becoming aware of these life lessons and transforming from them, you can prevent recurring patterns and promote personal growth.

One thing that helps restore balance, peace, and healing is looking at old journals and seeing how you resolved a particular issue. Say you experienced a loss and wrote how you felt. After seeing how you approached that feeling, you can then manifest the healing you used for a new situation or struggle that is similar. Returning to the journal entry helps you see what you did to feel better and invites you to practice it again.

Sometimes, you might feel overwhelmed by sadness, shaken by the state of the world and the growing division between people and nations. It can be hard to shake the weight of that sadness. In search of comfort, you turn to some old family journals. One entry catches your eye: a handwritten title that reads, *Why can't we love like the hippies? I don't care what people say.* It triggers an unexpected laugh and a warm smile.

In that moment, you see the person behind the words — and you see the hippie movement in a new light. Beyond the clichés of free love, you recognize it as a response to war, a celebration of music, poetry, nonviolence, and a deep longing for love — exactly what your heart is yearning for in today's world.

Looking back to a simple sentence in a journal entry made you smile and possibly have hope in a movement for change. It's a reminder that our personal contributions, no matter how small, can make a difference. It helped us shift our disappointment back into a peaceful balance again and feel good about ourselves and the contributions we can make.

Journaling is a powerful tool for self-reflection. It invites you to delve into your thoughts and feelings, and gain a deeper understanding of yourself. It brings you back to the what, when, and how, and the benefits of what you can bring into the now, and what you can leave in the past. The present is all there is. What do you want your future to be filled with? Journaling helps you answer this question and guides you on your journey of personal growth.

As mother and daughter, our relationship has been a close and respectful union joined at the hip, yet mindful and respectful, with space for independence. We care. We live. We love and experience fun in all the stages of our lives.

In our first interview as Strategic Ladies, we were asked two straightforward questions : *What are your fondest memories as mother and daughter?* and *What is the secret to your relationship?*

We looked at each other and paused, reflecting deeply. It wasn't that we couldn't find an answer — it was that so many memories flooded our minds at once, it was hard to choose just one.

Jai responded thoughtfully, *"The most significant moment was when I was still with my mother, being present and letting go of the world around me. We don't always have that luxury, but it makes all the difference when we do things together and are truly present in the moment."*

You see, our journey of self-reflection and personal growth is ongoing. It's rooted in the practice of noticing and remembering meaningful moments — something we nurture often through conversation and journaling. Reminding ourselves of these shared thoughts and memories is a vital part of our bond. You can never do it too much.

That interview stays with us as a pivotal memory, a reminder of what truly matters. We've both learned that transformation always begins within, and that the real work is in remembering — both the good and the hard stories — that have shaped us into the best versions of ourselves.

This act of remembering, of honoring our personal and shared journeys, is one of the key ingredients to a meaningful life and strong, lasting relationships.

We have found that spending time in silence and time with our foundation of faith is when we find the true joy of life and the true joy in our transformations. That's when we started to realize our purpose and enjoy life. The *"Now"* is where we create time with our children, grandchildren, friends, animals, and those in need. There is solitude in silence and just being.

True transformation starts with you, and you must always keep yourself in mind through your transformational journey.

Ready to start the journey again? Revisit Day 1 and uncover more about yourself and the healing that comes with mediation.

About the Authors

STRATEGIC LADIES BELIEVE THAT you can grow by harnessing the power within you and identifying where you are in the three selves. The process involves resolving inner conflicts and aligning the three selves before entering into each Situational Meditation practice. This understanding empowers you, instilling confidence and self-assurance in your journey of personal growth.

(1) The first is the *Fighting Self*, the inner voice that often undermines our confidence and diminishes our power. It's the self that we need to recognize and overcome.

(2) The second is the *Acknowledging Self*, the point at which one accepts oneself and gains an understanding of oneself.

(3) The last is the *Chosen Self*, where one harnesses the above powers to reach the desired self.

Our Manifesto is not just a *plan of action* but rather a *call to action* to just being. Knowing that each person's fights, acknowledgments, and chosen paths are different makes each person's Manifesto uniquely beautiful and personal. We each have one; it takes harnessing the power within to release it.

ABOUT DR. ESTELLA

Dr. Estella Chavous is an experienced educator, communicator, global marketer, and wellbeing consultant. Estella has significant professional experience in education, sales, and marketing, working in strategic leadership positions for Fortune 500 companies, including Abbott, Amgen, Bristol Myers-Squibb, and Schneider-Electric. Her marketing and people team experience includes domestic work in the pharmaceutical, biotech, and software industries and global assignments based overseas. She has built and led effective teams throughout her career, designed and implemented successful strategies, and developed and managed diverse programs, ranging from sales and marketing initiatives to employee wellness programs, enabling the transformational process.

Dr. Estella Chavous is deeply committed to education and knowledge sharing. As an Adjunct Professor at *UMass Global and Chandler-Gilbert Community College*, she imparts her wealth of experience and expertise to the next generation of professionals. Her dedication is evident in her teaching of various business, international business, marketing, and professional studies courses. Dr. Estella is also an Insight Timer Meditation Trainer (https://insighttimer.com/) and the co-host of Edge God In (EGI)(https://edgegodin.com/), and the voice of Emotional Intelligence in Christ (https://emotionalintelligenceinchrist.com/) which she co-founded.

Dr. Estella is not just an educator and consultant, but also a visionary entrepreneur. As a co-owner of *Strategic Ladies* and the *Mindful Media* show, she has demonstrated her leadership and commitment to the health and well-being of self and others. Her multifaceted skills are showcased in these ventures, which focus on making a positive impact. Dr. Estella has also authored several books, including *Situational Meditation: A Guide to the Theory and Practice of Meditation*, the *Situational Meditation Journal*, a Christ-filled assessment, and a booklet.

About Dr. Jai

Dr. Jacinta Chavous-Kambach (Dr. Jai) is a best-selling author, magazine columnist, Intuitive Relationship & Intimacy Coach, speaker, and diversity advocate. Her passion, experience, and education allow her to use her skills and gift of intuition in her business and writing.

Dr. Jai holds a Bachelor of Arts in Communication from *California University San Marcos*, an M.B.A in Organizational Psychology and Development from *American Intercontinental University Los Angeles/London*, and an Educational Doctorate in Organizational Leadership from *Chapman University System*.

She is the co-host of the *Strategic Ladies Mindful Media Show Radio Show,* an adjunct professor, and an avid reader and writer. She is the co-author of the bestseller book, *Situational Meditation: The Theory and Practice of Meditation*, which gets to the grit of meditation and how it can positively impact one's life.

Dr. Jai is a published BMI singer and songwriter who has worked with many accomplished artists. She has written with Emmy award-winning songwriter Janie Lidey and has debut singles, "I Know You Want Me" (https://music.youtube.com/watch?v=tOiEOyUbaTc&list=RDAMVMtOiEOyUbaTc) and "Hyperventilate" (https://music.youtube.com/watch?v=Lqw-3ZP-wHMM&list=RDAMVMLqw3ZP-wHMM), co-written with Paul Hines, an award-winning artist who collaborated with Teena Marie, Michael Jackson, and Debarge. She won the title of Ms. Egypt in the Queen of the Universe Pageant 2016, winning the title and trophy of best smile.

Cheeky, intuitive, and free-spirited, Dr. Jai loves life, reading, writing, and connecting with people. She also admits to her love for elephants and antiques.

www.ingramcontent.com/pod-product-compliance
Lightning Source LLC
Chambersburg PA
CBHW061735120626
46550CB00005B/1799